Generative AI

Research and Innovation for Professionals

RIVER PUBLISHERS SERIES IN COMPUTING AND INFORMATION SCIENCE AND TECHNOLOGY

The "River Publishers Series in Computing and Information Science and Technology" covers research which ushers the 21st Century into an Internet and multimedia era. Networking suggests transportation of such multimedia contents among nodes in communication and/or computer networks, to facilitate the ultimate Internet.

Theory, technologies, protocols and standards, applications/services, practice and implementation of wired/wireless networking are all within the scope of this series. Based on network and communication science, we further extend the scope for 21st Century life through the knowledge in machine learning, embedded systems, cognitive science, pattern recognition, quantum/biological/molecular computation and information processing, user behaviors and interface, and applications across healthcare and society.

Books published in the series include research monographs, edited volumes, handbooks and textbooks. The books provide professionals, researchers, educators, and advanced students in the field with an invaluable insight into the latest research and developments.

Topics included in the series are as follows:-

- Artificial intelligence
- Cognitive Science and Brian Science
- Communication/Computer Networking Technologies and Applications
- Computation and Information Processing
- Computer Architectures
- Computer networks
- Computer Science
- Embedded Systems
- Evolutionary computation
- Information Modelling
- Information Theory
- Machine Intelligence
- Neural computing and machine learning
- Parallel and Distributed Systems
- Programming Languages
- Reconfigurable Computing
- Research Informatics
- Soft computing techniques
- Software Development
- Software Engineering
- Software Maintenance

For a list of other books in this series, visit www.riverpublishers.com

Generative AI

Research and Innovation for Professionals

Sudha Jamthe

Business School of AI, USA

River Publishers

Routledge
Taylor & Francis Group
NEW YORK AND LONDON

Published 2026 by River Publishers
River Publishers
Broagervej 10, 9260 Gistrup, Denmark
www.riverpublishers.com

Distributed exclusively by Routledge
605 Third Avenue, New York, NY 10158, USA
4 Park Square, Milton Park, Abingdon, Oxon OX14 4RN

Generative AI: Research and Innovation for Professionals / Sudha Jamthe.

Foreword: Prof. Ahmed Banafa
Book Website: http://generativeaibook.org (follow here for up-to-date tech stack and resources)
Book hashtag: **#GenAIBook**

Routledge is an imprint of the Taylor & Francis Group, an informa business

ISBN 978-87-438-0813-8 (hardback)
ISBN 978-87-438-0818-3 (paperback)
ISBN 978-87-438-0815-2 (online)
ISBN 978-8-743-80814-5 (ebook master)
DOI: 10.1201/9788743808145

Dedication

Neha, my rock

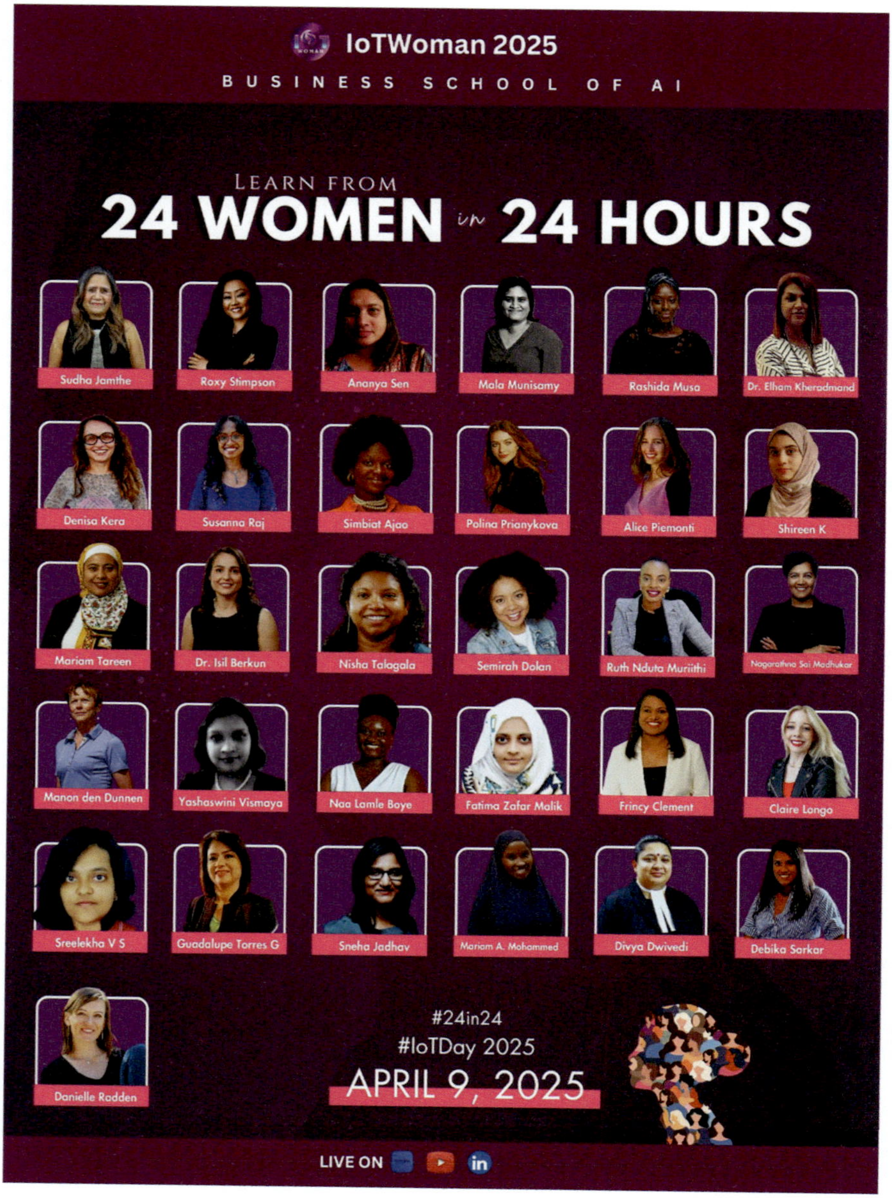

Figure Sudha Jamthe's community of change agents who inspire her to keep finding futuristic technologies and innovation opportunities to build technology for an ethical, inclusive world.

Contents

Foreword

Artificial intelligence stands at the forefront of technological innovation, revolutionizing how we work, create, and connect. Among its most groundbreaking advancements is Generative AI—a field that not only mirrors human creativity but also pushes its boundaries further. Sudha Jamthe's exceptional book encapsulates this transformative journey, providing an insightful and practical guide to understanding and harnessing the vast potential of Generative AI.

This book bridges the gap between the intricate technological underpinnings of generative AI and its practical applications in the real world. Sudha skillfully demystifies complex topics such as foundation models, attention mechanisms, and diffusion techniques, presenting them in an accessible way for readers of diverse backgrounds. Beyond the technical aspects, she explores the transformative impact of Generative AI across industries, offering a clear roadmap to leverage its capabilities in business, education, and beyond.

What truly sets this book apart is its unwavering focus on responsibility. Sudha does not shy away from tackling critical ethical issues and societal challenges posed by generative AI. She thoughtfully addresses topics such as bias, job displacement, and intellectual property, encouraging readers to approach this powerful technology with accountability and inclusivity at its core.

Sudha's deep expertise, paired with her clear and engaging writing, ensures this book is not only informative but also transformative. Whether you are a seasoned technologist, an industry leader, or simply curious about the future of AI, you will find this book to be an invaluable resource.

As we stand on the brink of an AI-driven future, this book provides the knowledge and vision necessary to navigate its complexities and embrace its opportunities. It celebrates the achievements of generative AI while offering a thoughtful guide to ensuring its responsible development.

I am honored to introduce this compelling work and invite you to delve into the profound insights it offers. Together, let us envision and create a future where generative AI uplifts and benefits everyone.

Prof. Ahmed Banafa
Award-Winning Author
Professor at San Jose State University

Preface

Five years ago, on a Monday evening, I remember teaching my Autonomous Vehicles class at Stanford Continuing Studies, teaching about building a RoboTaxis. My innovative students wanted to build mobility services for everyone and asked me how to get a self-driving car to talk to visually impaired people to help them in an emergency. I love teaching the depths of technology and getting my students to ask questions to arrive at cool innovations. At the end of this class, we found that all real products for all their ideas could only be built with lots of data and by creating artificial intelligence models that were trained with the data. And we needed a newer approach for AI to add voice to the car. The generative AI of today did not exist then, but our search to innovate toward it had begun.

This led me to teach an Artificial intelligence boot camp as my next course at Stanford Continuing Studies to find gaps to innovate for my students to push the limits of AI past what existed then.

The pandemic hit, and I had to switch my first AI class to Zoom. Imagine teaching on Zoom to hundreds of students from around the globe. The chat was on fire. The students had brilliant questions and were interested in AI in every possible industry.

I have written seven books that have served as textbooks for my students. In alternate semesters, I research and engage with real industry practitioners. So for the past five years, I have been writing and teaching and publishing books and research and doing industry advisory about machine learning and computer vision, what are now known as traditional AI.

One such AI was natural language processing (NLP). It was used as a voice assistant in Alexa and Google Home. I did projects with my students at my student community at the Business School of AI. I made a fun video for my students, showing Google Home and Alexa talking to each other. It was hilarious because Alexa would say, "Ask me anything," and Google Home would ask her a question, and Alexa would forget the context and get all confused. Google Home would do the same. This was because conversational AI was in its infancy with the NLP technologies till 2022 when generative AI was born but became mainstream Innovate toward or innovate towards. This brought chatbots like ChatGPT that can retain context and continue to chat with us in long conversations.

Another problem that existed in training AI was the need for lots of data. Imagine training a factory robotic arm to watch a manufacturing factory for quality control. Lots of data was needed, covering all possible defects in all possible lighting and positions. An engineer named Ian Goodfellow solved this data problem by creating synthetic data using a generative adversarial network (GAN)(Goodfellow et al., 2014) where two neural networks trained each other with one trying to create an image of a person and the other validating if it was indeed a face. OpenAI built upon this to create Image-GPT, where an AI model could predict the finish of a full image when it was shown only part of an image. This became the precursor to today's GenAI models generating images and videos.

In October 2022, I hosted an online session at the Business School of AI, teaching about foundation models, BERT and GPT models comparing them with machine learning. ChatGPT was launched the following month in November 2022 and a million people chatted with it in a week. Conversational AI has finally arrived.

I began writing my GenAI book immediately and got it ready as the class textbook for my class in Spring 2022 at Stanford. As I taught the class in March at Stanford, each week, an innovation was launched in the GenAI space. I had to adapt to bring the latest to my class. Google launched Lambda, which later became Gemini. GPT 3.5, which powered ChatGPT, was expanded to GPT 4.0 as a multi-modal model. Prompt engineering became a hot new field. As I taught professionals of all backgrounds, I found no-code GenAI tools such as AgentGPT, which evolved to building Agent AI. The Kindle book I wrote for my class and the expanded course content became the seed for this book.

As more innovative professionals wanted to innovate with AI, I have taught GenAI and Agent AI courses to 100K learners in LinkedIn Learning. I have taught EMBA consortium leaders from around the world to innovate with AI and GenAI in Ferrari cars and E-commerce sites alike. I have taught girls to build language translations for refugee women in Africa.

As the GenAI space has been growing with innovations, two competing forces are at play. Technology companies of all sizes are competing and innovating to expand the GenAI models, APIs, and tools, adding more jargon each and every day.

The second factor is the realization that GenAI has been built with content from the Internet without data consent, creating ethical issues and copyright lawsuits, and business risks. There has been research published about the ethical side of GenAI and creative ways to solve this from tons of new research being published daily.

This creates a world of hype and research to sift through that intimidates even the smartest minds. So naturally, like a bear that rushes to put out a fire in a forest, I am drawn to demystify the jargon and help my learners understand what is hype and what is real so you can find their place with your innovation.

I set out to build this GenAI book to demystify the hype, educate you on the innovations, and shed light on the latest in research help you figure out where the gaps are to innovate.

I am excited for you to get a solid foundation on GenAI technologies with Responsible AI and learn the latest in research to expand the world of Conversational AI to bring ethical, creative, and value-creating use cases to everyone.

I welcome you to the world of GenAI. I cannot wait to hear a RoboTaxi talk to me to tell me how to sit back and relax as it takes me to my destination. I am excited to watch what you build using Responsible GenAI in your world to expand traditional AI to generate a world of possibilities.

Welcome to the Era of Generative AI

Generative AI has expanded the world of traditional AI with large language models (LLMs) reaching linguists, artists, screenplay writers, marketers, and technologists alike while being challenged by ethicists and policymakers, leading to an expanding field of Responsible AI.

AI writes poetry and marketing copy. AI generates images. AI generates code. AI chats like a human, retaining the context of conversations. This generative AI is real today. Like all new technologies, it promises the future. It is disrupting industries and raising questions about how much to believe the NLP hallucinations. ChatGPT has become a poster child for generative AI scaling to 100 million users in the first 2 months of its launch, faster than any technology of the past. As a technology futurist, I am excited about this wave of technology because of its promise and also about its limitations. I am not here to teach how to code with generative AI. I am here to demystify the possibilities for everyone. I am here to help you, the innovator, to find your place in it.

Generative AI is the evolution of foundational AI models, a search by AI researchers to create multi-modal AI systems to go past prediction from data to extrapolate to generate new possibilities. It is the promise of the new business model in the technology industry with the API economy. It is a strategic inflection point in the technology industry, creating reverberation across the entire technology stack of the software industry.

It is fueled by the proxy war among tech giants for domination in revenue generation in the promise of artificial intelligence. Microsoft has invested in OpenAI with its GPT series of models and integrated generative AI into search, challenging Google, who owns 96% of the global search market. Google retaliated with Bard, which later got renamed to Gemini model and Palm models with deeper integration into enterprise office product, a 96% market owned by Microsoft. What is the actual cost of a search vs chat? How can you make sense of this beyond the hype that is heightening each day?

For the developer, it is a technology war between which is better, transformer-based models or general adversarial network (GAN)-based approaches to building AI that generates content.

It is calling upon product innovators to build middleware products to build integrations upon these APIs to shift the ecosystem with more products to create a new landscape of opportunities. It has inspired innovators to create a new field of tech called prompt engineering. It has brought in lawyers with questions about who owns the generated content. AI learning has woken up educators to redefine what learning means for humans. Business leaders who were building AI pilots with huge volume of data from enterprise for predictive models are given another slew of tech jargons and how amazing the next tech model coming out of today is over all their machine learning investments without clarity on how enterprise data can be used by generative AI and what is the business imperative of this shift. Industry 5.0, with connected products and factories, is evolving with the human-centric design of AI systems with chatbots impacting all functional areas of business.

I am here to demystify generative AI technologies to help you understand the models and APIs in simple English.

I am here to help you understand how you can build products using generative AI and how product managers are needed to shape the evolving space.

I am here to help lay out the ecosystem of generative AI and help you make sense of the key drivers and types of players so you can play a key part in vertical or horizontal shifts of the space and use no-code AI to engage confidently to create partnerships, pilots, and new business models.

I am here to help everyone looking at this space to understand the social, ethical, and legal ramifications. I will ask questions and expect you to jump in with more well-informed confident questions as you read further chapters of this book.

I hope that we will find answers together. My job here is done if I can spark your imagination to discover gaps to innovate, bringing your business acumen, and passion for your world. We begin a journey to come together to make AI finally work for all of us and not benefit a few at a cost to some of us.

Who is This Book for

This book is a primer, an introduction for product managers, business leaders, technology enthusiasts, and AI ethicists interested in learning the depths of generative AI technology, ecosystem, and the shifts in landscape. This is a book for the non-coding business leader who wants to understand the depths of technology and how different technology models are getting interconnected to strategically build out opportunities and shifts in industries, markets, and economies.

Who is This Book NOT for

This book is for the engineer who wants to understand the big picture of where generative AI technologies fit in. This is not a book for the developer or data scientist who wants to build generative AI using code and wants help with understanding the models and how to program them. This is not an explanation of ChatGPT. This is not a technical book on how to build generative AI.

Read on if you want a clear understanding so that you can draw inspiration on what is your place here so you can decide for yourself what you can and want and will be able to do with it.

What You Will Learn in This Book – Details, Lots of Details

Section One: The Technology

Learning Objective:

At the end of this section, you will be able to understand the top models of generative AI space. My aspiration for my readers is to confidently compare models from competing companies and ask smart questions about the models with a focus on innovating using AI. Since my main focus is to ensure we go past the hype and posturing by makers of any particular models, I have chapters about prompt engineering and NLP hallucinations. Again, these are explained with zero coding so you can understand how to use the models with confidence and know when to trust them and when to challenge the promise of any technology vendor. Then, based on your level of programming, you can develop the models with a language of your choice or call the APIs or develop use cases for your company using no-code.

I have added in a reference appendix, several research papers related to these models for those of you who want to go deeper into understanding particular models. This will also help you understand which of these models are in open source and which are built as walled gardens by specific technology companies so you can make an informed decision when you choose to build upon a specific model.

Section Two: Product Management and Business

Learning Objective:

In the business section, I lay out the shifting landscape of generative AI companies big and small. You can learn about where funding for generative AI is focused with billion-dollar valuations. I have provided an analysis of AI search space to help you understand the cost of a chat transaction vs the cost of a search to get you to think about how to make business sense of the media coverage. Like I always remind my Stanford students, I want you to go past the posturing of ecosystems to understand the business drivers and what is expanding the market. I want you to understand what industries and businesses have the potential to be cannibalized by generative AI models. If you focus on the enterprise, I want you to develop the confidence to come up with whether you want to build generative AI in the cloud or core.

Finally, I want you to understand the API economy and shifts in business models. My approach is not prescriptive, so you can innovate as a business leader to create new business models and partnerships.

Section Three: Societal Impact

Learning Objective:

In this section, I teach product managers the evolving middleware layer in the generative AI space. Product managers will learn how to build API products with a solid understanding of key concepts such as NLP hallucinations and prompt engineering. Product designers will develop an understanding of designing human-centric design products where the customer is not a passive stakeholder but actively engages in designing the AI solution. This is a huge shift from product design measuring engagement as the key metric in the data economy.

This section teaches about the ethical and legal aspects of this evolving technology and how humans humanize AI, and how to see past its obvious mistakes.

Learners will understand ethical issues if building this technology on the data of artists of the GitHub code of software engineers without their consent. There are many open questions about how some people see ChatGPT also bringing equity by democratizing information while others are taking the time to show where it is hurting people asking for it to be governed. My job is to lay out the facts and get you to think. I leave it to you to decide how you want to utilize this information to build ethical AI.

Finally, this section calls on product innovators to find gaps to innovate to build new products in this new space. We focus on the shift in the software engineering industry tech stack so product managers can rearrange the stack by verticalization of the space or create new fine-tuned models for specific customer segments.

Conventions and Legends

I have a callout for you to innovate like this in every chapter. It looks like this:

Call for Innovation:

Throughout the book, you will see my futuristic take on several areas of generative AI. You will see me make futuristic predictions of where I see the trends evolving to shift the ecosystem or a threat or futuristic use cases but I have taken care to remind you that the space is in nascent stages and it calls you the innovator to fill in the gaps from your knowledge and passions so these are opportunities for you to innovate for your career or areas of passions.

Feedback

We consider your feedback a gift. We have taken care to provide accurate information and edited the book, but if you find any errors or if you want to provide feedback or related reference that we can include in a future release, feel free to email sujamthe@businessschoolofai.com

References

Goodfellow, I. J., Mirza, M., Xu, B., Ozair, S., Courville, A., & Bengio, Y. (2014). Generative Adversarial Networks. ArXiv. https://arxiv.org/abs/1406.2661

Acknowledgments

It all began with my students, it always begins with my students. Thanks to the 15,000+ students who have taken my AI course at Stanford and LinkedIn Learning or the digital transformation leaders who have learnt AI ethics from me at Barcelona Technology School and Business School of AI, and the several visiting EMBA and MBA groups who have learnt how to create value from AI. You got me onto the AI journey and led me to foundation models. My special thanks go to Manon Den Dunnen from the Amsterdam Police Department for her session about synthetic data in mid-2021. This was an eye-opener to think about generated data beyond those used to augment training data for machine learning models and autonomous vehicle simulations. Manon introduced this topic right, with the right balance of excitement and ethical questions. I have carried that balance into my research.

I am thankful to Ken Herron for being a believer in my potential to be authentic while chasing my purpose. I am thankful to IoT council Rob Van Kranenburg, Ken Sinclair, and several others for entertaining my endless questions and discussions about AI.

My students who come together for IoT Day Woman and Weeklywed Speaker Series at the Business School of AI, you keep me on constant research and learning to answer your questions. I did a presentation in 2021 about foundation models and a quiz about what are the characteristics that led me to dig deeper to learn, and that learning has not stopped yet.

Thank you, Susanna Raj, for getting me into Inclusive AI research, and for Suresh Lokiah and Yashaswini Viswanath, for partnering with me on research papers.

Thank you to my students and peace negotiator Aishatu Gwadabe for raising the question about how to get Hausa language, a low-resource language, to be included in language translation models, which led me on a quest to understand language models in 2020. Your questions and Susanna

Raj's leadership led me to co-found Global South in AI to make language models more inclusive and bring new researchers to NeurIPS since 2022.

Thank you to all the 50+ language poster researchers of Global South in AI @NeurIPS. Your questions always led me to be curious and ask questions of my own, and we have just begun the journey to bring language AI with all its generative aspects and text modalities to solve problems in your countries, and seeded the writing of this book to explain language models in simple English to engage more people to learn generative AI. Special thanks to NeurIPS for a special grant to get me and the Global South in AI (NGO) team on a journey to apply generative AI language models for gender equality to build a new Language AI curriculum to train girls from global south countries to create translation models for low resource language and claim their space in the world of Language AI.

Thanks to my friends in Brazil, Thiago Felipe Avanci, for his contribution to help me understand the Portuguese language's place in the language AI world. Thanks to my friend Dr. Ricardo Baeza-Yates for translating my Autonomous Vehicle talk in Spanish for a Chilean conference and inspiring me to learn Spanish to understand the reality of many Spanish language variants between Spain, Mexico, and Latin America. Also, for your fantastic explanation of the state of large language models.

Leah Giannantonio, you have inspired me with your generative images on Twitter, and your passion and belief in prompt engineering has got me on a journey to include prompt engineering. I am grateful to Robert Schwentker for your friendship and shared curiosity, which helped me develop my original Generative AI Tech stack picture, which has evolved with growth in GenAI models.

I always believe that feedback is a gift, and it is doubly special when it comes from my readers. Irene Shamkova took the time to proofread the book and send me feedback. I am thankful for your generosity and insights.

Thanks to my daughter Neha for holding me whenever I stopped for a breather as I questioned my crazy endeavor to write a living book that kept expanding each day and making me think about the moral ramifications of AI. You believed more in me than I believed in myself in those hours.

Thank you to my student and AI researcher, Yashaswani Viswanath, for the initial research papers about AI Ethics in the GenAI space. Responsible AI in the GenAI space has evolved with so much research in the sustainable building of models to fairness and explainability and is still an important area ripe for research.

Thank you, Manon Den Dunnen, for writing the foreword for the original Kindle version of this book and for Prof. Ahmed Banafa for the foreword and for trusting my work before the world could see it. Thank you Sourav Rout for indulging my discussion about Industry 5.0 and human agency in human-centered design using intelligent chat apps.

Thank you, Tashfeen Mahmud, for editing my Kindle book as my Stanford student who was an innovator, community builder, and writer, expanding my horizons of GenAI to think about ethics and innovation as two sides of the same coin.

Thank you Debika Sarkar, my editor and AI Ethics Program Manager who works closely with courses to ensure AI ethics is reflected well. My words reflected my thoughts and became clear passages and lessons in this book because of the magic dust you sprinkled.

There are so many more who have contributed to this book and my journey in AI research as innovators in my community online or as my students or my friends and believers. Thank you, you know who you are.

To my Mom, the believer in my potential, my work and my passion to connect the world to share knowledge and demystify technology for all and to bring down the patriarchy by making AI ethical. I am nothing without you. This book is dedicated to you.

List of Figures

List of Tables

List of Abbreviations

NLP	Natural language processing
GAN	Generative adversarial network
BERT	Bidirectional encoder representations from transformers
GPT	Generative pre-training transformer
LLM	Large language model
NGI	Next Generation Internet
SEO	Search engine optimization
SEM	Search engine marketing
LSTM	Long short-term memory
RNN	Recurrent neural network
LaMDA	Language model for dialogue applications
PaLM	Parallel language model
Sea-Lion	Southeast Asian Languages In One Network
OALL	Open Arabic LLM leaderboard
RAG	Retrieval-augmented generation
ReAct	React with action
ReWOO	Reasoning without observation
KI-NLP	Knowledge intensive NLP
MAU	Million daily active user
SLA	Service level agreement

1

Generative AI

Abstract

This chapter gives an introduction to generative AI with several examples. It covers three important topics to help you get started with learning GenAI. One is that you will get the big picture of why we need GenAI. Second is the GenAI tech stack and ecosystem that teaches you all the different technology layers of GenAI with the ecosystem of key technology players. The third outlines its impact on business, industries, and ethics to help you understand how GenAI is being applied in different industries so you can see the big picture of creating impact from the technology. Also, in many of the chapters, there is a state of research to help you get a balanced view between innovation and future research directions on this field. The goal is not only to help you learn GenAI but also to get clarity on where you can contribute on the innovation or research side.

1.1 What is Generative AI

Do you ever think about how we are communicating with generative AI every day? Every single time we type a text message on our phones or social media messaging app as you type a word, an AI gives us an option for the next word by guessing the next word. When we chat with a chatbot, it does this to build out full sentences. This is generative AI at work, with a "next best word algorithm", always guessing the next word from a neural network in its memory. This neural network is made of billions of connections of words connected to more words trained to understand the semantics of language and nuances of how words are related to other words. Generative AI is artificial intelligence that is available today for us to give simple prompts in text or voice for AI to generate new original content. This can be in several modalities, such as text, images, videos, 3D, voice, music, or code.

DOI: 10.1201/9788743808145-1

I was surprised to find out that when you connect to a video streaming platform for a meeting, an AI tool takes your photo and sends it to the cloud. For the duration of the meeting, it generates your image as a good guess instead of spending expensive bandwidth to stream your face repetitively for an hour-long meeting. This image generation is available to create new images that can become fake images or creative for your next marketing campaign or presentation.

Music, art, and videos can all be generated by AI, though not to the quality of a creative person, but you still hold the superpower of prompting it to say what you want the AI to generate. Let's be clear: this AI does the technicality of digitizing voice and sounds and cannot capture the art behind art. As we learn more about generative AI, we will learn how this prompting works, and you have an opportunity to create a human-augmentation of AI to make it work for you instead of taking your work away.

1.2 What is the Generative AI Ecosystem and Tech Stack (2025)

The ecosystem is evolving with large tech companies and several startups and existing players in cloud, search, enterprise, and chip space all creating integrations and fine-tuning of models to build up the generative AI tech stack.

Join me in looking at this from the figure below, starting from the foundation models at the bottom. Remember, our goal is not to list every single company in this space. We want you to understand the different layers of technologies and how they connect to the next layer for you to figure out how you can innovate to create new startups or technologies or contribute to open source or use this to understand how as an enterprise leader you can bring your data to create fine-tuning and integrations to create intelligence applications to solve customer problems.

1.2.1 Understanding the generative AI tech stack

See Figure 1.1.

1. There are foundation models at the bottom. There are only a few because it is expensive in terms of GPU power needed to train large language models (LLMs) for text or large diffusion models with a huge number of images. Training a foundation model is based on the concept of attention by adding billions of parameters to create a matrix of numbers from the data so the AI knows how each word or section of an image

GENERATIVE AI TECHNOLOGY STACK				
VERTICAL SOLUTIONS				
	Art	Design	Movement	
	Education	Business	Finance	Law
	Government	Healthcare	Media	Publishing
INTELLIGENT APPLICATIONS				
	ChatGPT	CodeWhisper	BARD	Bloom
	NeevaAI	CoPilot	Chinchilla	ChatSonic
MLOPS				
	Token Cost	Versions	Training Costs	Cloud vs Core
MIDDLEWARE				
INTEGRATIONS	Zapier	Cloud	WordPress	Messag
	Data source	Cross-platforms	Email	Slack
FINE TUNED	Text summarization	Q&A	Knowledge Mgt	Video Creation
	Image generation	Style Transfer	Language Pattern	Image to Photo
RESPONSIBLE GENAI				
	Data Privacy	Fairness	Inference Scaling	Inclusion
	Security			
RAG	Simple RAG	Agentic RAG	RAG with Reinforcement Learning	
MODALITIES				
Text	Image	Audio	Video	Code
LLM FOUNDATION MODELS				
Closed Source			Open Source	
GPT/OpenAI			Stable Diffusion	
LaMDA/Google			HuggingFace	
Claude / Anthropic				
(C) Sudha Jamthe 2023-2025			Follow generativeaibook.org for updated versions	

Figure 1.1 Generative AI technology stack.

is important relative to others. This creates the training model. This is fine with unlabeled data using unsupervised learning. This is what is available as an API. These foundation models are not re-trained because it is expensive. For example, ChatGPT is trained by a foundation model GPT3.5, which was trained in September 2021, so its information is limited to that date. GPT3.5 was fine-tuned and optimized for specific tasks, such as question-answering and text generation, to create new vertical layers.

2. These foundation models could be further divided into proprietary closed platforms or open source models with the source code in open source.

3. The next layer is the fine-tuning needed to create a middleware tech layer. This is where the model is trained using a small set of labeled data using supervised learning. If it is created as a middleware, it is available with its API and again can be a closed platform or open

source. An example of this stable diffusion model is the foundation model with scribble diffusion built upon it to allow image creation using scribble as input additional to text. Another example is the riffusion model, also built upon stable diffusion. Riffusion takes the image generated as a spectrogram and generates music as the output.

4. The next layer involves fine-tuning the model further to create intelligent applications. This is the intelligent application layer on top of a horizontal intelligent application. All the possibilities we see with ChatGPT and now with Gemini are in this intelligent application layer. So it is easy to think of this as a chatbot talking to us that retains context and continues to chat to fetch information, answer questions, or write essays. This is where prompt engineering plays a very critical role. If you are using your proprietary data, one choice is to keep the data in the prompt and prompt the model to generate code or run the prompt to fetch answers. A simple example of this could be to let the model do some data analysis for you or generate code for further data work. Or simply chat with the chatbot. This is called an intelligent application because the chatbot creates an instance for every chat with a user and retains the context of the chat. This is where you can continue a conversation with ChatGPT or Gemini, or Copilot as a continuous chat thread, and it retains the context of your conversation. You build this intelligent app by fine-tuning to set guard rails for the app, and that is done by labeling training data. For example, here is where ChatGPT will show its limitations and developers set boundaries and refuse to turn racist or refuse to think beyond fetching information and creating the poems, stories, or letters that you want it to write. Professor Losh from the College of William and Mary pointed out that this limitation of ChatGPT does not allow for critical thinking and limits itself to safe answers. ChatGPT refuses to apply critical thinking to prompts beyond just fetching facts from its memory.

5. Another layer of custom applications is evolving on top of intelligent applications. This calls for innovation in different industries, team situations, and the chatbot experience you want.

6. A new layer of applications evolving on top of intelligent applications is cross-platform intelligent apps that sit on top of multiple foundation models. One example of this is Nova – AI chatbot, which combines ChatGPT and GPT 3.5 Turbo. We will be seeing more such cross-platform apps across Open AI, Gemini, and other open-source platforms.

7. A tools category of foundation model is evolving, allowing for building upon one or more open source or foundational models offering an AI infrastructure. One example of this is Hugging Face. It provides pre-trained models and builds a community of developers who contribute to open source. It specializes in getting models to production faster with a process called distillation.

See Figure 1.1 to understand what makes up the generative AI technology layers and how they are interconnected to each other. This is not a map of an ecosystem of companies and their interconnection. This is meant to be a map for the product manager or the enterprise business data owner to understand what different technologies in the generative AI space offer and how they connect to the next. This can serve as a guide for you to understand where you want your company to play or what you need to buy for a pilot to use your data to create the Intelligent Application that promises innovations with use-cases you aspire to bring to your company. In this figure, look at each layer and see if you want to operate at that layer or want a partner there or where value is created by generative AI for your business.

1.3 What is the Promise of Generative AI

Why is generative AI different from artificial intelligence, which has been generating excitement (no pun intended) for the past decade? Generative AI, by virtue of its underlying technology, has the capability of learning from a vast volume of unlabeled data and then transferring this learning to a small set of labeled data for specific applications or new languages by a process called "semi-supervised learning." We will learn the English version of these technologies in Section One.

This large volume of data is our world of information on the Internet, books, and the lived truths of our cultures that are getting digitized around the world or in our voice communication and movement as we move around the world and are captured by cameras and sensors. So Generative AI promises to do two things for us – one is that it helps us gleam knowledge from this vast volume of data of our history and communication and knowledge stored in business documents. Second, it generates new content from this learning instead of finding historical data from its training. This opens up a world of possibilities, from chatbots that can understand our intent and continue conversations to language translation models that generate new texts for languages it has not been trained before and to generate images and art from our prompts, bringing our wishes to life and so much more left to your imagination.

It is important for you not to think about GenAI as a tool only for writing your resume or building your slide deck for a presentation. When you think of innovation, there are bigger promises, such as sifting through various patterns to create potentially new materials, life-saving vaccines, or totally new designs. Material discovery is an evolving new area of innovation with Gnome from DeepMind (DeepMind, 2024) and MatterGen from Microsoft (Microsoft Research, 2024). The promise lies in expanding what we believed as possible to expanding the world to solve problems.

1.4 Why Does it Matter?

This generative AI is a strategic inflection point in industries and in society compared to past incremental technologies that were built by engineers and iterated by product managers and marketers to reach specific customer segments to create and scale businesses.

It is creating a shift in technology infrastructure with the high cost of data centers costing energy and water.

It is creating a shift in the software development stack with AI generating code, challenging the work of software engineers.

It is creating a shift in business models from a data economy to an API economy.

It is impacting industries not just by driving change in processes and tools but in how AI should be creating value from combining GenAI with traditional AI.

It is shifting society in fundamental ways with questions about how we learn, communicate, and grow as humans.

Generative AI is promising to create content mimicking art and chatting like a human mimicking language. This is a big shift from past technologies, which is raising questions about the creativity process and humans' need and ability to create art. The automation that comes with an AI that chats like a human is raising ethical questions about what we need technology to do for us and creates fear about whether it can replace humans. People whose jobs are impacted by such AI are challenging the productivity aspect of AI while technologists excited about an AI that can write and talk like a human are pushing the boundaries to build reasoning into the AI.

Traditional artificial intelligence, such as machine learning, was trained by historical data and made predictions to solve problems. These were problems that were waiting for technology to improve processes, create efficiencies, and generate revenues. This is a language businesses understand and could adopt with new waves of technologies. But generative AI does not solve the problems that we were waiting for. The AI consumes a large volume of data and has an almost human-like comprehension (or so it appears) of the intent of users and situations and generates content. It challenges our education systems in how we teach learning to our young people. If it is about perspective writing, a generative AI chatbot can write your essay or research paper. This has prompted many universities to ban students from using ChatGPT, an intelligent application based on generative AI models, to write their homework. Today, students chat with ChatGPT and fetch answers in university classes. So, educators are challenging students to go past fetching answers from the Internet to apply the class learning in creative ways. This is being seen in journalism in articles written by ChatGPT too, to go past information to deeper insights by experienced humans.

This is a huge change that is threatening to some who do not understand the depths of capabilities and limitations of these evolving technologies and is exciting educators like me to rethink how we teach and how to bring the learning into a partnership in the learning process to educate them by using their creative thinking and empathy which are uniquely human traits.

This technology seems surreal because large technology companies are competing with each other with an urgency to innovate to capture market share in the overall AI market.

As you read, you will get comfortable with the technologies and the reality of where the technology capabilities exist to make more informed decisions about adapting these generative AI technologies meaningfully.

There is a brewing debate about whether generative AI in art and music is making people less creative or whether it will replace the jobs of writers and artists. I am in the camp that AI is still a tool and will augment the work of writers and artists to focus on their strengths in the creative process. Also, I believe art will exist as long as we as humans have feelings.

1.5 What is the Impact on Business Markets and Industries?

Business users are concerned about use cases from generative AI impacting their businesses, shifting the ecosystem of players, and the pace at which this hype of emerging technology will go past the trough of disillusionment to impact their business and the billion-dollar question of who will win and what to bet on for them to build out their business applications. I will be covering these in detail in Section Two to show the business drivers and teach you how to make sense of this shift and how to influence it to your advantage to enhance your business and career.

Figure 1.2 Gartner's Hype Curve for emerging technologies for marketing from mid-2022. Image source and credits: Gartner

I am referring to the Gartner Hype Curve for emerging technologies (see Figure 1.2), which is a framework we use in the technology industry to keep track of which new technology is a hype and is going to go away or which technologies are going to scale in 2 or 5 years or longer.

Do you see generative AI for marketing climbing up to the top of the hype curve? Well, marketers are early adopters of AI because they have huge volumes of customer data from their campaigns, behavioral data, and post-sale customer support data. Marketers also have budgets to acquire new customers or reduce churn and retain existing customers, all with secrets buried in data. So marketers began using AI to apply to their campaigns to understand which channel a customer will click next. For example, when you plan a campaign for a new market, the earlier approach would be to segment customers and send them a campaign for a particular channel, such as an email, an ad, a postcard, or the old-fashioned phone call. Marketers began piloting "Next best action" algorithms that allow them to understand which channel each customer will click next with an AI predicting this to guide their campaigns for better conversion.

The "next best word algorithm" a chatbot uses to guess the next word to generate has a different underlying technology called transformers as compared to the "next best action," which is based on machine learning predictions. But marketing began demanding learning the next best word in chatbots and inadvertently created a business imperative for AI-generating content in chatbots that became the front-end for customer interaction on websites. This happened in 2021 and seeded the business justification of generative AI while the research on large language models continued in parallel, feeding into this world of chatbots that are now at the top of the generative AI adoption excitement.

I want to share another topic from recent news showing billion-dollar technology companies competing with each other for our attention and challenge you to think about this differently so you can make sense of the business impact of these technologies and their apparent speed of scale to the mainstream.

Microsoft has invested $10B in OpenAI for ChatGPT and integrated GPT models into Bing search as the "new Bing." Google started with Bard and evolved to new Gemini models competing with OpenAI and ChatGPT. This created a PR frenzy of search engine wars powered by Generative chatbots in early 2023. In early 2025, DeepSeek-R1 (Guo et al., 2025), a reasoning model, was launched in open-source and with a new technological approach that costs less to build and run the foundation model. I call on you to think critically about how this technology is going to contribute to revenues in search markets and other markets that you are involved in.

If you are a business person investing $10B in a new technology that you are acquiring from OpenAI, how would you measure the ROI of that investment? It has to convert to revenues in multiples of $10B. So the promise is to integrate ChatGPT into Microsoft products. Is search the best product for this integration? Will it affect revenues from search?

Let us think through this. If ChatGPT is integrated into the "new Bing" and offers a context-aware chat interface so people will be engaged to chat on Bing search, it will increase consumer engagement. However, the revenue model of search is from the links from searches that send people to websites that pay for these visitors because they are relevant customers to their business. Some of these customers come organically, which is called search engine optimization (SEO), and some of these are paid keywords that businesses bid on to get the users to be sent to their sites instead of their competition's site. This is search engine marketing (SEM). This is where Google, Microsoft, and Yahoo make their revenues.

As of January 2025, Google's global search engine market share was at 78.83%, with Bing following at 12.23%, Yandex at 2.94%, Yahoo at 3.07%, Baidu at 0.77%, and DuckDuckGo at 0.87% (Statista citation). Can ChatGPT shift this by creating a better-engaged chat-based search for Bing over Microsoft? The important question to ask in that case is how this will translate to revenues from SEM, which is based on the PageRank formula that sends relevant search results to the right websites. I am not asking you to take sides with one tech giant over another. I am urging you to think critically about why Microsoft made the $10 billion investment in OpenAI. I am urging you to think strategically past the PR news to think about potentially new business models that you can create from chat-based searches to create the new SEM for revenues from businesses who are downstream from your search chats.

Later in this book, I will teach you how generative AI models work so you can get a clear understanding of the power and limitations of this technology and see how you can create new business models strategically by thinking beyond what you read in news to think about building technology products, utilizing your enterprise data to model AI and to think creatively about new business models for value creation as the industry shifts from this new technology changing the industry layout and software ecosystem.

Let's dive in!

References

Guo, D., Yang, D., Zhang, H., Song, J., Zhang, R., Xu, R., Zhu, Q., Ma, S., Wang, P., Bi, X., Zhang, X., Yu, X., Wu, Y., Wu, Z. F., Gou, Z., Shao, Z., Li, Z., Gao, Z., Liu, A., . . . Zhang, Z. (2025). DeepSeek-R1: Incentivizing Reasoning Capability in LLMs via Reinforcement Learning. ArXiv. https://arxiv.org/abs/2501.12948

DeepMind. (2024, March 5). Millions of new materials discovered with deep learning. DeepMind. https://deepmind.google/discover/blog/millions-of-new-materials-discovered-with-deep-learning/

Microsoft Research. (2024, March 11). MatterGen: A new paradigm of materials design with generative AI. Microsoft Research. https://www.microsoft.com/en-us/research/blog/mattergen-a-new-paradigm-of-materials-design-with-generative-ai/

SECTION ONE

Technology

2

Technology Foundation Models

2.1 State of Research of Foundation Models

As you get ready to learn about the technology of foundation models, remember the two sides of this coin: innovation and research. Innovation calls for fresh ideas, new ways of living, and doing business excites us to dive into the world of new possibilities.

Research, on the other hand, reminds us of the gaps and challenges. Think about GenAI responsibly to understand its impact on people and earth resources and where we can truly innovate to bring the promise of this technology to our world.

Transformer architecture initiated a change in how neural networks were built. They helped create a new set of AI models known as foundation models with the ability to pre-train AI with a very large volume of information. This created the potential to train foundation models on all information that has ever been created in the world. Such an AI could extrapolate that learning to generate more knowledge, creating the world of generative AI (GenAI).

Transformer architecture came from a Google research paper, "Attention is all you need," (Vaswani et al., 2017) where an AI was taught the concept of attention. This allowed the AI to learn the relationship of words to other words within a context window. The size of the context window could be a sentence, a paragraph, or a whole chapter of a book. This powered foundation models the ability to create natural language conversations that retain context, allowing for human-like conversations in intelligent chatbots.

The only caveat was how the foundation model research evolved. Instead of getting all the world's knowledge, foundation models were built by a small set of companies who focused on the English language only and

DOI: 10.1201/9788743808145-3

looked to the Internet for content regardless of who owned it or whether it was a decent language. This created the foundation models we have today, limiting their potential and calling for more research to make it live to its full potential to get us an AI that can learn all the information of the world and extrapolate that learning to generate more content to help all humanity solve problems that have been left unsolved.

So, as we embark on learning GenAI, you have the potential to build a limitless AI or one close to that promise if you focus your research on ethical principles of data ownership, privacy, and inclusion.

Let us now look at how research has evolved from here and where the opportunities are for you to innovate and contribute to the research going forward.

2.1.1 Synthetic data and deepfakes

Synthetic data is the term used to describe data created by an AI. Originally, this was created by a method called general adversarial network (GAN), by which an AI generates an image by talking to another AI to validate the generated image. With foundation models, this has evolved to generate content of all types. This has created new opportunities to create synthetic data to allow for training data to train AI easily. This has also created an ethical challenge of creating a category of fake faces and fake voices of people known as deepfakes.

This technology of generating fake faces to appear like celebrities and fake voices of real people is raising ethical questions about permission to use look-alike images of people in ads. This is challenging the entertainment industry by creating fake voices, impeding voice actors. Deepfakes with GenAI have created new deepfake videos that are primitive in nature but are contributing to misinformation (Vaccari & Chadwick, 2020).

2.1.2 Environment cost of foundation models

The growth of foundation models comes at a cost to the environment (MIT News, 2025). Pre-training large volumes of data requires expensive GPUs to build foundation models. This training costs power and water in data centers. People are waking up to the environmental cost of training and running these models. Much research is needed on how to create transparency on the cost of building AI based on such foundation models that cost for pre-training, launching models, and when it runs inference every time, and to create benchmarks to compare against the benefits from such AI. The environmental cost is obvious so innovation is needed to figure out alternatives that do not have such hefty environmental costs.

Foundation models have enabled the promise of generative AI, but calls for a better approach to training without a huge cost to the environment, transparency in ownership of training data used, and to create of a multi-modal, multi-sensory experience, getting AI closer to the real world.

The purpose of this chapter is to set the foundation of the concepts to understand generative AI and to get a simple non-code explanation of generative AI models. This is not a technical explanation of how to build using these model APIs; that is not the purpose of this book. Our goal here is to serve leaders from various fields impacted by generative AI to understand it with enough depth to figure out how it impacts them, where the opportunities are, and what they can do as the technology ecosystem shifts with the iterative innovation of generative AI technologies.

For readers interested in the research behind the models, I have provided references to understand the various papers and concepts that led to the development of the models to where we are today. You can get a holistic understanding of concepts and models to proceed to learn about the product, business, and societal implications of generative AI without any coding or technology prerequisite.

2.2 What Are Foundation Models?

The foundation model was a term introduced to define a set of deep learning models (BERT, DALL-E, GPT-3) that were trained on very large datasets. They applied transfer learning to homogenize tasks with capabilities in language, vision, robotics, reasoning, human interaction, and technical principles such as model architectures, training procedures, data, systems, security, evaluation, and theory with applications in law, healthcare, education, and societal impact of inequity, misuse, economic and environmental impact, legal and ethical considerations (Bommasani et et, 2021).[1] These models are now called generative AI, though that concept began much earlier with GANs, which we will see next. Foundation models were so named because other models can be built upon them downstream.

Several models have evolved related to the foundation model research. For those interested in the multiple research papers, you can look at https://github.com/criteo-research/iclr_analysis for an ICLR conference paper on

[1] https://arxiv.org/abs/2108.07258

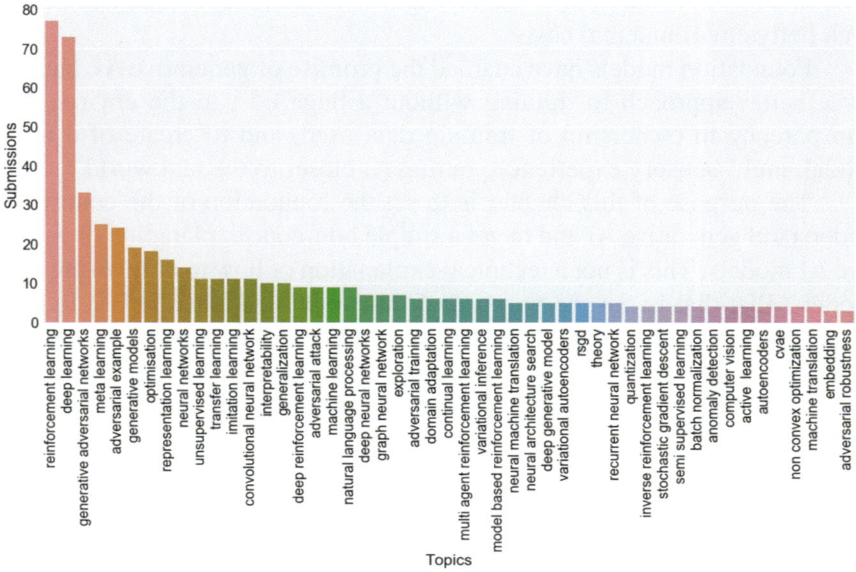

Figure 2.1 1449 research papers from the ICLR 2019 AI conference analyzing the frequency of submitted topics.

the topics covered in research papers, as each element of the research was developed into better models (Figure 2.1).

Microsoft has released a foundation model called Visual ChatGPT, which is a ChatGPT-like text generation model that combines visual image generation in one. Now GPT-4 and Gemini have the text and visual capabilities in one foundation model and have become multi-modal models, setting that as the new standard to build GenAI models to support all modalities in the same models.

2.3 Generative Adversarial Networks (GAN) and Synthetic Data

Generative adversarial network (GAN) was introduced by Ian Goodfellow in 2014. A GAN is an AI model talking to another AI model in an adversarial mode to help improve each other toward a goal. To understand this, let us look at how a computer looks at an image. For us humans, an image, say a photo, is visual with colors and layers of content, and we can easily see a face or multiple objects in an image.

A computer stores an image as a matrix of numbers where each of the values represents a pixel value. The pixel value is the intensity of the image as a number between 0, which represents black, and 255, which represents white. Thus, an AI sees an image as a matrix of numbers. Hence, a GAN tries to change the pixel value to create images till it gets the adversarial AI confirming that it has indeed generated an image as it was expecting.

The first GAN published had an AI that could recognize a face and another AI that created a matrix of numbers to create or generate an image of a face and fed it to the first AI. The first AI would be adversarial and critique the second AI on not creating a good enough image and reject it with a low confidence score for drawing a face. The second AI will take this input and try to improve the matrix numbers to generate a new image and feed it back to the first AI. This will repeat till the second AI generates an image that is acceptable to the adversarial AI.

This was the beginning of generative AI for images. This was called synthetic data and was used to generate images to use for training data for images. This also, unfortunately, has led to the proliferation of images that are now fake and led to the growth of fake media from generated images, videos, and voices.

2.4 Attention Mechanism and Transformers

Large language models (LLMs) created neural networks trained on a large set of data (words) and focused on the prediction of words. Google introduced BERT trained on 345 million parameters to predict the next best word and expanded this to the Gemini model that is comparable to OpenAI's GPT-4 model. You can see this prediction in Google Search (see Figure 2.2). A variation of this is masked language prediction, where the word is in the middle of other words if predicted. In all large language models (LLMs), the training data was a large dataset of data typically from the Internet, and this was unsupervised training, meaning the data was not labeled; hence, this process was called pre-training. Also, when we go past simple texts to a full language dataset, known as Corpora, language is treated as a collection of words without any consideration of the difference between languages and the cultural contexts it carried that the entire world of Linguistics has created and researched. This is called word embedding. This became the limitation of LLM models that are trained focused on word predictions.

The most common model used to build LLMs was the long short-term memory (LSTM) model, and it essentially attempted to chat by making

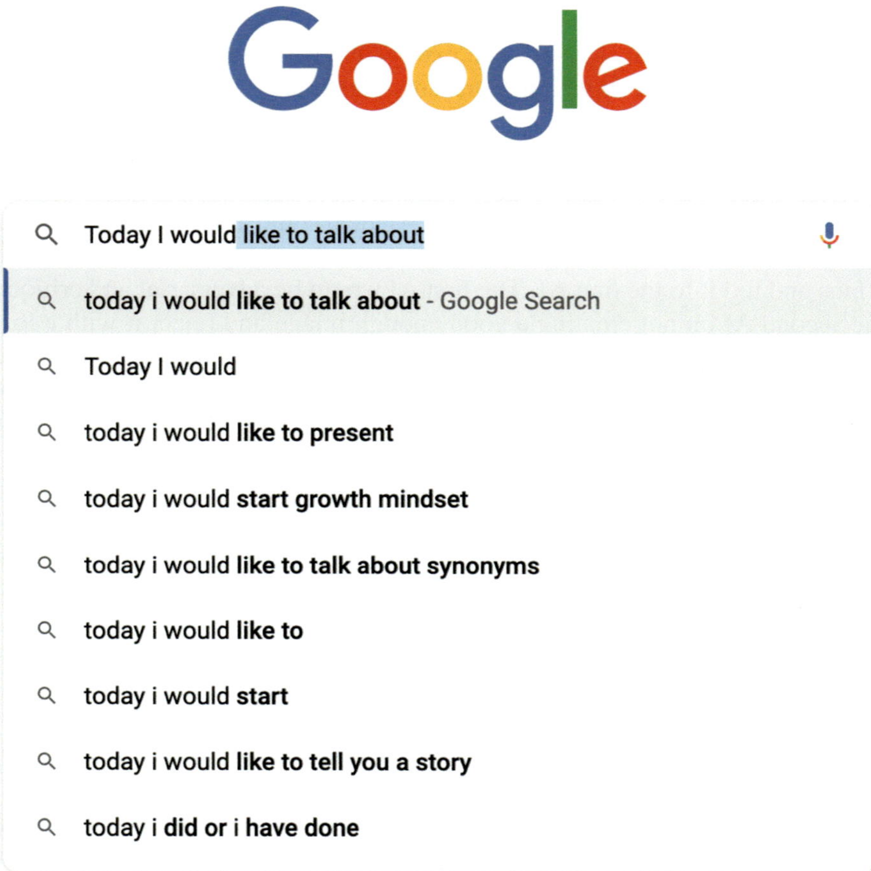

Figure 2.2 Google Search shows the BERT model making the next word prediction (taken on Feb 17, 2023).

sentences by guessing the words that came next or in the middle of a sentence without much ability to understand context.

Much research has been done on LLM language data about word embeddings and the biases they propagate. For example, this research showed word embeddings that propagated gender bias against women (see reference section for citations).

Google Brain researchers introduced a revolutionary concept called “Attention” (Vaswani et al. 2017) that introduced a new model type called “Transformers” which replaced RNN and convolution neural networks with a mechanism called “Self-Attention.” The model looks at words relative to words adjacent to them and also looks at the frequency of usage of words in a language dataset. This allows the large language model (LLM) to learn faster by adjusting the weights it gives to each input based on the location of a word in a document and enhances language models to get the meaning of the language texts.

OpenAI launched generative pre-training transformer (GPT) models with GPT-1 trained with 1 billion parameters (2018) and fast forward to GPT-3 trained with 170 billion parameters in 2020. This was trained with 570 GB of Internet websites, books, and articles. This came with an API interface to allow developers to query the model to create downstream applications that are foundational models about which we were talking.

All GPT models have a self-attention mechanism of transformers with an encoder for input and a decoder for output, which does masked language modeling to fill in the missing words to form sentences with meaning to generate language texts that are closer to language. They take in tokens, which are words or groups of words, and build vectors by assigning a number to each word in the sentence based on its importance. This allows the model to understand sub-meanings and complex relationships of words in language.

Before large language models (LLMs) with transformers that had self-attention, natural language processing (NLP) models created chatbots by listing users' intent and planning a chat path for a conversation for it. Now, GPT models advanced natural language processing by automating conversational AI, but it has some limitations. These are some of the limitations of ChatGPT:

1. It is not transparent, so when you chat with a GPT-based chatbot like ChatGPT, you cannot know how it arrived at a particular answer.
2. It does not understand the user's intent.
3. It will not follow a user's explicit prompt and does not help write more imaginative sentences beyond what it has in its learning.
4. It can be toxic or share biased content from trained data from the Internet, which carries biases of everyone in the world.
5. The biggest problem is that it can offer NLP hallucinations, which are semantically proper sentences that are misinformation or absurd sentences caused by the AI losing focus on keywords that give it meaning. We will cover AI hallucination in detail further in this chapter.

Following GPT, OpenAI launched ImageGPT, which made predictions on pixels similar to words and generated images.

Another improvement over GPT was InstructGPT. This took user input into the training process and preserved user intent.

The much talked about ChatGPT is built upon InstructGPT, and hence, it offers a chatbot application that is content-aware of user intent within a session. We will review ChatGPT in detail under intelligence applications that are built upon the AI models.

Hugging Face is an open-source model development online community to democratize machine learning and transformers.

I will be explaining several foundation models throughout the book. I want to call out important models and approaches to explain the model in English so it helps us understand the competitive landscape, your business choice of what model you pick to fine-tune your business or build products upon to create new middleware, and more.

1. Zero-shot learning: One semi-supervised learning or transfer learning algorithm is called zero-shot learning. It pushes the boundary of AI as it exists today by extending what is known to extrapolate to unknown situations. This is used in new language translations for languages without feeding translation data for the new low-resource language.

2. BERT is a language model that predicts the next best word to auto-generate words. This is used in search engines to understand the context of words in both directions and hence is good for translation tasks.

3. GPT-4 builds upon GPT-3 to support multi-modal support for text and image. But fundamentally, GPT is a generative pre-trained transformer. GPT is a single-directional context learner and is good at context-aware chat conversations within a session. GPT powers Microsoft's chatbot efforts and is embedded into Bing search.

4. LaMDA stands for language model for dialogue applications, which is also a transfer-based model and powers Google's Gemini and other applications. While GPT was trained on Wikipedia and Internet data, LaMDA was not trained on the open Internet and is focused on human-like dialogue.

5. PaLM stands for parallel language model and is from Google and is a text generation model focused on large-scale language tasks.

6. Diffusion models are also transformer-based and focused on the concept of attention (which we'll learn in detail further in the book) but generate images by adding noise to images and reducing the noise in some areas to add clarity to generate images. This has become the foundation of

most image generation models until NVidia came with the StyleGAN series of models that generate images using the GAN concept of general adversarial network with two AI models training each other to generate synthetic content such as an image.

2.5 Diffusion Models for Images

Large language models are built using a transformer model where the AI creates a mental map of words and their relation to other words based on how often they are used. The underlying technology is a neural network, which is like many layers of connected neurons, and the AI learns by going over the layers to glean more information from its training data.

Let's try to understand this using the next best word guessed in a search engine like Google. You can also test this in the auto-correct on text messages on your mobile phone. The AI generates the next word by guessing what it should be based on what the rest of the sentence is. To train this chat AI, the training data must have been many sentences. The AI takes each sentence, collects the words, and makes a matrix of it by learning what the ending of each sentence is and its relation to the previous word in the sentence. Now, how does it know which word in each layer of its neural network is important? That is a value called weights. How does it know what learning should propagate into the next layer of its neural network? That is a value called bias. These weights and biases are built from the billions of parameters we hear about in each of the large language models. Running the neural network through billions of these parameters is very expensive during training, costing GPU processing power. That is why we have very few foundation models powering the promise of generative AI coming from a few large technology companies.

See Table 2.1 for how many billion parameters were used to train the top language models.

Table 2.1 lists the number of parameters used in training of top large language models.

Why does it matter how large the number of parameters on which the LLM was trained is? The large language models are trained with all possible data with these huge numbers of parameters. Then, they are used to build BARD (not called Gemini) or ChatGPT-like intelligent applications built upon models like LaMDA or GPT. The higher parameters make the models more robust to transfer their learning to new tasks like answering questions or text generation. This is why there is competition among the foundation models on using more parameters. They can build a model supporting more

Table 2.1 The number of parameters used in training of top large language models.

Model name	Number of parameters
BERT	345 million
NLLB-200	54.5 billion
LaMDA	137 billion
GPT-3	175 billion
PaLM	540 billion
GPT-4	175 trillion parameter
Gemini	1.586 trillion parameter
Minstal	7 Billion
Gemma (open source light Gemini)	1B, 4B, 12B and 27 Billion versions
DeepSeek-V3	671 billion parameters
ERNIE 4.5	1, 10 and 100 billion

Table: ERNIE model architecture. Adapted from Hugging Face (n.d..), "ERNIE – Transformers Documentation," retrieved from https://huggingface.co/docs/transformers/en/model_doc/ernie.

applications and better use cases. The big downside of this competition is that an increased number of parameters means large processing power, which costs energy to train these models. That is a huge downside to foundation models because of their sustainability cost on the planet.

So I hope this gives you an idea about what the number of parameters means when you compare foundation models and choose them, questioning the value of what bigger promises better transfer learning for upstream usage at a steep cost to the environment.

> **Call for Innovation:** We need innovation to think of a different approach to make large language models smarter instead of just throwing more processing power at the models.

References

Bommasani, R., Hudson, D. A., Adeli, E., Altman, R., Arora, S., Von Arx, S., Bernstein, M. S., Bohg, J., Bosselut, A., Brunskill, E., Brynjolfsson, E., Buch, S., Card, D., Castellon, R., Chatterji, N., Chen, A., Creel, K., Davis, J. Q., Demszky, D., . . . Liang, P. (2021). On the Opportunities and Risks of Foundation Models. ArXiv. https://arxiv.org/abs/2108.07258

Goodfellow, I. J., Mirza, M., Xu, B., Ozair, S., Courville, A., & Bengio, Y. (2014). Generative Adversarial Networks. ArXiv. https://arxiv.org/abs/1406.2661

Vaccari, C., & Chadwick, A. (2020). Deepfakes and Disinformation: Exploring the Impact of Synthetic Political Video on Deception, Uncertainty, and Trust in News. Social Media + Society, 6(1). https://doi.org/10.1177/2056305120903408 (Original work published 2020)

MIT News. (2025, January 17). Explained: Generative AI's environmental impact. MIT News. Retrieved March 18, 2025, from https://news.mit.edu/2025/explained-generative-ai-environmental-impact-0117

Vaswani, A., Shazeer, N., Parmar, N., Uszkoreit, J., Jones, L., Gomez, A. N., Kaiser, L., & Polosukhin, I. (2017). Attention Is All You Need. ArXiv. https://arxiv.org/abs/1706.03762

3

Generative AI Models Explained

3.1 State of Research of Generative AI Models

We have learned earlier about the inner workings of GenAI models. Generative AI models are not different from past AI models in that they are also built as neural networks. They take in training data to learn and create millions of layers of neural networks to build out the model.

The main difference between traditional AI such as machine learning is that generative AI models are built as semi-supervised learning models as a combination of a pre-trained unsupervised foundation model and a supervised model fine-tuning the last layer of the neural network. Research in GenAI models has focused on making the models more accurate and creating multi-modal models combining text, audio, and video in the same models.

1. **Big models with large parameters:** The growth of GenAI models lies within the hands of a few large technology companies because of the extensive investment needed to pre-train these models. This has created a focus on expanding research and development on increasing parameter size with the belief that the more parameters, the better the learning accuracy of the foundation model. We will learn what parameters are and how they contribute to the accuracy of learning the underlying neural networks of the foundation models. But I believe that research and development should go past building bigger models to smarter, smaller models that solve real problems that humanity needs. The technology world is divided by increasing parameter size in foundation models. While Intel launched Aurora GenAI with 1 trillion parameters, Microsoft launched Phi-3 as a small GenAI model that can run on a phone (Abdin et al., 2024). Apple has launched Apple Intelligence foundation models with 3 trillion parameters to run efficiently on devices (Gunter et al., 2024). So the world of research is open to both small and large models

DOI: 10.1201/9788743808145-4

and new approaches to leverage on-device and cloud approaches for GenAI foundation models.

2. **Multi-modal models:** Foundation models were originally created for a single modality. Text-based models for language, audio models for voice, and diffusion models for image generation. With GPT-4 and Gemini, the models became multi-modal with the ability to generate multiple modalities of output in the same model. Multi-modal models bring a convergence of NLP and computer vision to bring us closer to real-world interaction, where we receive input from multiple sensors, extract information, and make sense of the world around us. Earlier visual embeddings were converted to text embeddings, so LLMs were able to understand only texts. But with Gemini, the pre-training was done with a universal embedding for multiple modalities without the need to convert to text for audio or images right from the start (Gemini Team, Google). With a multi-modal model, you can extract text from images or ask questions about an image. For example, using Google Gemini on Vertex AI or GPT4, you can show an image with words and pictures in a scenery and ask the model to extract names of streets or words from an image. Or you can input an image and ask the model to continue to have a conversation about the object seen in the image. See Table 3.1 below for a list of current models, explained in simple English.

Much work remains to make GenAI models work for various applications involving a variety of data sources. We will learn more in future lessons about how to extend GenAI models to learn from extended data sources in a privacy-preserving way using an approach called RAG in future lessons.

3.2 What is Model Modality?

Modality is the sensory method by which we experience the word. In AI, modality is the mode of content generated by a generative AI. A chatbot that receives text and outputs text is said to be in text modality. An image generator like Midjourney receives text and outputs an image in image modality. The different modalities are available as follows. We are beginning to move to the trend of multi-modal communications. Some recent models like GPT-4 are combining text and image to offer a multi-modal user experience in interacting with the AI.

- Text modality
- Visual modality

Table 3.1 Models explained in simple English.

Model name	Modality	Ownership
BERT	Text	Google
LaMDA	Text	Google
GPt 3 , GPT-3.5- turbo and	Text	OpenAI
NLLB	Text	Facebook/Meta
Flan-T5	Text	Google
DALL-E	Image	Open AI
GPT-Image	Image	Open AI
Imagen	Image	Google
ERNIE-ViLG	Text to image	Baidu (Chinese)
Taiyi	Text to image	OpenSource (Chinese)
Different Dimension Me	Image to anime	Tencent
Stable Diffusion	Image generation	Stability AI (Open Source)
Midjourney	Image generation	MidJourney
Codex	Code generation	OpenAI
GPT-4	Multi-modal	OpenAI
MusicLM	Music	Google
PaLM	Text	Google
Gen-1	Style transfer across videos	Runway.ai
GauGAN, Style GAN	Image style transfer	NVidia
ControlNet	Built upon stable diffusion and adds controls to image generation	Open source built upon stable diffusion
BLOOM	BigScience large open-science open-access multilingual language model	Hugging Face and 1000 AI researchers
NeMo LLM	Service for fast LLM deployment to the cloud	Nvidia

- Code generation
- Voice modality
- Multi-modal

3.3 GenAI as Semi-supervised Learning

The foundation models are trained using vast unlabeled training data. These are later fine-tuned by doing training again with a small set of labeled training data to build out the middleware and intelligent applications like ChatGPT.

3.3.1 Foundation model generating code and its business implication

Codex is a foundation model trained on code from GitHub and other public sources of code, and it generates code.

So it is obvious that this has an implication on software development and for students learning to code. One risk of these models is that they violate the ownership of developers when generating code from their training. Also, there is no easy way to validate that this code generated is, in fact, accurate and does what it is promoted to do.

3.3.2 Impact on enterprise industry

Generative AI can create very innovative intelligent applications that business people should think about carefully before bringing them to their enterprise.

First, let us take a step back into the world of AI before generative AI. Machine learning models were trained using vast volumes of labeled data as supervised learning to look for patterns in historical data to make predictions and recommendations for business for various industries, functions, and applications. When the volume of data was too vast, they used deep learning with unsupervised learning to train to look for patterns and make predictions. An example of this is DeepMind using historic medical records from NIH in the UK and applying deep mining to predict eye and kidney diseases for preventive healthcare.

Now, let's look at the technology of generative AI. Foundation models are built by a combination of unsupervised learning with a chat volume of data, and then a small set of data is applied as semi-supervised learning for specific areas of functionality or languages, etc. This is left open-ended to solve for the functionality of text summarization or Q&A, etc.

So why not apply this generative AI technology principle as semi-supervised to recurrent neural networks (RNNs) with enterprise data? Yes, that is doable.

You can use generative AI to help you make predictions and generate answers where traditional machine learning has hit a roadblock with your available data. You could use the machine learning model as a pre-trained model and build semi-supervised models to generate predictions with your company data, which you can pilot and test for your business.

One example of a company doing this is in finance.

Citadel is a finance investment hedge fund company that has integrated GPT 3.5 into Schrödinger AI by getting code generated and using it to make predictions for market trading opportunities beyond what their machine learning models could predict. Of course, as we learned about NLP hallucinations, there need to be checks to validate the reality of predictions.

References

Abdin, M., Aneja, J., Awadalla, H., Awadallah, A., Awan, A. A., Bach, N., Bahree, A., Bakhtiari, A., Bao, J., Behl, H., Benhaim, A., Bilenko, M., Bjorck, J., Bubeck, S., Cai, M., Cai, Q., Chaudhary, V., Chen, D., Chen, D., . . . Zhou, X. (2024). Phi-3 Technical Report: A Highly Capable Language Model Locally on Your Phone. ArXiv. https://arxiv.org/abs/2404.14219

Gunter, T., Wang, Z., Wang, C., Pang, R., Narayanan, A., Zhang, A., Zhang, B., Chen, C., Chiu, C., Qiu, D., Gopinath, D., Yap, D. A., Yin, D., Nan, F., Weers, F., Yin, G., Huang, H., Wang, J., Lu, J., . . . Ren, Z. (2024). Apple Intelligence Foundation Language Models. *ArXiv*. https://arxiv.org/abs/2407.21075

Gemini Team, Google. “Gemini 1.” *Google AI Blog*, Google, 6 Dec. 2023, storage.googleapis.com/deepmind-media/gemini/gemini_1_report.pdf.

4

LLM – Large Language Models

4.1 State of Research of Large Language Models (LLMs)

Large language models are the fastest-growing area of generative AI with a focus on training with words and language in pre-training. The most common applications are intelligent chatbots that predict the next words to form sentences to have a conversation with humans. Now, they are evolving from building chatbots to automating using autonomous agents.

Here is how LLMs have evolved over the past decade (see Figure 4.1).

Large language models (LLMs) have become multi-modal, as we have learned in earlier chapters.

LLM research is now focused on building reasoning capabilities into LLMs. The big open research question is whether AI can reason like a human. For example, Agent AI is deployed in factories to get sensor data from the environment to reason and make automation for safety. Agent AI does reasoning of human clicks in marketing and support situations to ensure that customers get time-sensitive information in hotel bookings and medical access.

What is reasoning?

Let us take a step back and understand what reasoning is.

Generally speaking, reasoning is the analytical thinking to make decisions based on some information. Abstract reasoning is the ability to work with abstract concepts. I remember a past colleague who was proud of his son questioning an abstract concept like numbers in math by asking her what the number 6 meant. Abstract reasoning requires identifying patterns and trends, making sense of formulas, and making connections between concepts, ideas, and objects.

Abstract reasoning also involves examining situations from multiple perspectives.

DOI: 10.1201/9788743808145-5

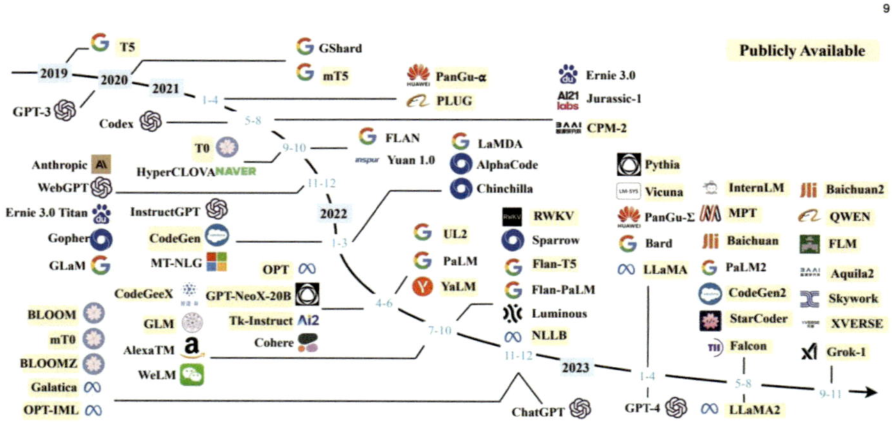

Figure 4.1 A timeline of existing large language models (having a size larger than 10B) in recent years. The timeline was established mainly according to the release date (e.g., the submission date to arXiv) of the technical paper for a model. (Credit: https://arxiv.org/pdf/2303.18223)

What about logical reasoning?

Logical reasoning is a way of thinking to solve problems, make predictions, and come to conclusions. So naturally, the engineers who were building AI were reminded of algebra and math and built math benchmark datasets to test the reasoning power of LLMs. I believe that reasoning by analogy or understanding multiple perspectives is not limited to math problems and can be seen in humanity in critical thinking skills in writing, too. OpenAI-oi from OpenAI and AlphaProof from Google Deepmind take a similar approach to defining reasoning by proving the new models perform better in math problems using a benchmark math problem set known as GSM8K.

In a recent paper titled "GSM-Symbolic: Understanding the Limitations of Mathematical Reasoning in Large Language Models"—currently available as a preprint paper (Mirzadeh et al., 2024)- Apple researchers have taken the GS8K math dataset and expanded it to a dataset known as "GSM-Symbolic," where they made modifications.

Published in October 2024, they have shown by experiments that the LLM appears to be only making predictions and is not doing reasoning. One example in this research was to get an LLM to do simple math to count the number of fruits. When extra information such as the size of the fruit was included in the query, the LLM gave incorrect answers. So future research opportunities should address this question about the reasoning capabilities of LLMs with better benchmarks and could cover spatial reasoning. Also, reasoning is not limited to math, so new benchmark datasets should be built by humanities and liberal arts researchers to test LLMs on critical thinking.

4.2 How Large Language Models Work

Large language models (LLM) are neural networks built based on a transformer model trained on a larger dataset of words and focused on the prediction of words. LLMs are pre-trained on a corpus of language data. During training, LLM creates a mental map of words and their relationship to other words based on how often a word is used.

Tokens are the basic unit of training an LLM. Tokens are made of words or parts of a word and punctuations that make up a language. They serve as the building blocks of how an LLM understands and generates words to chat like a human. The next step in training an LLM is to create word embeddings. Since a computer can understand only numbers, word embedding is a number assigned to each token. They are different approaches to assigning a number per token and are generally available as a library. The next step in the training of LLM is to create vectors from the word embeddings. Vectorization is the process of creating word embeddings. This is done by the training process, where a vector or matrix of each word vector is mapped to other vectors. A vector database is used to store word embeddings. A vector database provides storage, retrieval, and search accuracy, so choosing the right vector database is important for the efficient operation of LLMs.

References

Mirzadeh, I., Alizadeh, K., Shahrokhi, H., Tuzel, O., Bengio, S., & Farajtabar, M. (2024). GSM-Symbolic: Understanding the Limitations of Mathematical Reasoning in Large Language Models. *ArXiv*. https://arxiv.org/abs/2410.05229

5

LLM for Global Languages

5.1 State of Research of LLM for Global Languages

Language models evolved from natural language processing (NLP) technologies of the 1970s with machine learning technologies with large language models. With the shift to attention-based models, text lent itself to large language models to train generative AI models.

Originally, LLM models were trained using Wikipedia and books focused on English. GPT-3 supports 95 languages with these six core languages: English, Spanish, French, German, Japanese, and Chinese. GPT-3 for world languages was developed on Hugging Face by researchers from around the world. These include GPT-3 SW for GPT Swedish language (AI Sweden, n.d.), GPT-3 for languages of India from AI4Bharat.org, and GPT-3 for African languages from Masakhane.

Aya open-source open research models and datasets: Cohere for AI runs an open research project that has launched a fully open-sourced Aya model and datasets. The Aya models are multilingual and support 101 languages. It was built from research contributions from 3000 global independent researchers from 119 countries. They have also built multilingual instruction fine-tuning datasets covering 114 languages.

One of the latest in multilingual models is the research about model merging in a multilingual perspective. When LLMs were originally built using English and Latin-based language data using Internet data, they were expanded to more world languages by fine-tuning the LLM with a dataset of instruction pairs for new languages. This failed in tasks for world languages because each language presents unique learning challenges to perform specific tasks. So, research from Aya has shown the objective-based and language-based merging of fine-tuned models (Ahmadian et al., 2024).

DOI: 10.1201/9788743808145-6

New datasets and small models: These are evolving for low-resource languages. InkubaLM (Tonja et al., 2024) is a human-translated benchmark dataset for 16 typologically diverse low-resource African languages covering three tasks: natural language inference~(AfriXNLI), mathematical reasoning~(AfriMGSM), and multi-choice knowledge-based QA~(AfriMMLU).

Language research remains a ripe area of research for everyone to bring their languages and local knowledge to extend the world of LLMs in many directions.

5.2 DeepSeek-R1

DeepSeek-R1 is an AI reasoning LLM model built on the latest innovative technologies of reinforced learning that was launched by DeepSeek, a new Chinese startup, DeepSeek. It became newsworthy for many reasons impacting enterprise (Automated Buildings, 2025).

1. DeepSeek costs almost 100 times less to build the model. It broke the myth that the only way to build AI is by throwing more data at it, thereby requiring more data centers.
2. DeepSeek costs less to run in inference so enterprises can build AI with less token cost.
3. DeepSeek published their approach and code in open source. This has opened the floodgates for every startup and innovator globally to build on the new model.

5.2.1 Impact on AI markets

Many tech stocks crashed in valuation because investors realized that a huge number of GPUs or large data centers were not required to build AI.

By putting their code in open source, DeepSeek has broken the stronghold of top tech companies from owning the AI foundation model space. Now, AI is accessible to everyone.

5.2.2 What is the impact on industries?

For enterprises to adopt a new technology, typically tools are built on top of innovation technologies, making it easy to build applications. This middleware layer is still missing for LLM space. Only LLM applications are intelligent chatbots for customer service.

Every time your customer chats with you for support or inquires about your product in pre-sales cycles, which is typically considered good for business, with LLM-based AI, it costs a token cost at inference.

5.2.3 What is the token cost at inference?

After you build AI, the production version of AI is called inference AI. With LLM, it costs an incremental cost called tokens every time you run your application, and each chat with the customer costs a small amount that quickly adds up. So, enterprise markets were not adopting LLM in full gusto because of the high token costs.

Now, DeepSeek has shown that their token cost is much cheaper.

5.2.4 Data privacy and security

DeepSeek is new to the market, and just like the first version of GPT3.5 that powers ChatGPT, it will go through iterations to adapt to enterprise-grade security and privacy protections.

But in the meanwhile, because DeepSeek shared their model code in open source, there are several startups offering hosted versions of DeepSeek. It remains to be seen if this will evolve to a Linux-like model with RedHat picking up market share offering enterprise grade SLA's building upon open-source software.

I believe that the opportunity is ripe for enterprise industry innovators to test out new LLM options that are cost-effective and secure and demand the overall AI market to compete to innovate to serve them better.

5.3 Mistral

Mistral was one of the first open-source LLMs that was created in France against proprietary LLM models like GPT and Gemini, claiming to democratize AI. Mistral NeMo is fully open-sourced under an Apache 2.0 license. Other Mistral models are not open-source.

5.4 Aya-101

Aya-101 is an open-sourced multi-lingual LLM model that was built by Cohere-for-All non-profit along with a collaborative team of 3000 global researchers from 119 countries contributing language instruction dataset for fine-tuning Aya to support 101 global languages (Üstün et al., 2024) and (Cohere For AI, n.d.).

5.5 Country-specific LLM

Several countries have created their language-specific LLMs with their language datasets. This will ensure that the LLM understands their culture and their local problems. Nigeria has created an LLM called Awarri (Dosunmu, 2024). Chile is working on LATAM-GPT, funded by their government in collaboration with local universities. Singapore has developed Sea-Lion (Southeast Asian Languages In One Network), a local LLM of 7 billion parameters trained using Southeast Asian languages Thai, Vietnamese, and Bahasa Indonesia (Tan, 2024) (AI Singapore, 2024). This LLM was built to allow AI to support multilingual Singaporeans to code-switch across Southeast Asian languages. There is a movement from several regions around the world to create local benchmarks to make LLMs work for global south languages and with accented English to ensure that the LLMs work in a culture-preserving way for the local application of LLM technologies. SEA-HELM is from the Singapore Sea-Lion team offering a benchmark for LLM evaluation for Southeast Asia region (AI Singapore). There are several Arabic LLMs given that Arabic has many dialects and is spoken by 380 million people. Hugging Face has an open Arabic LLM leaderboard (OALL) to compare the many Arabic LLM models (El Filali et al., 2024).

References

Automated Buildings. (2025, February). Demystifying DeepSeek for Enterprise. Automated Buildings. Retrieved March 18, 2025, from https://www.automatedbuildings.com/2025/02/demystifying-deepseek-for-enterprise/

Ahmadian, A., Ermis, B., Fadaee, M., & Hooker, S. (2024). Mix Data or Merge Models? Optimizing for Diverse Multi-task Learning. ArXiv. https://arxiv.org/abs/2410.10801

Tonja, A. L., Dossou, B. F., Ojo, J., Rajab, J., Thior, F., Wairagala, E. P., Aremu, A., Moiloa, P., Abbott, J., Marivate, V., & Rosman, B. (2024). InkubaLM: A small language model for low-resource African languages. ArXiv. https://arxiv.org/abs/2408.17024

Üstün, A., Aryabumi, V., Yong, Z., Ko, W., Onilude, G., Bhandari, N., Singh, S., Ooi, H., Kayid, A., Vargus, F., Blunsom, P., Longpre, S., Muennighoff, N., Fadaee, M., Kreutzer, J., & Hooker, S. (2024). Aya Model: An Instruction Finetuned Open-Access Multilingual Language Model. ArXiv. https://arxiv.org/abs/2402.07827

Lelapa. *Hugging Face*, https://huggingface.co/lelapa.

El Filali, A., 2A2I, Alobeidli, H., Cojocaru, R., Boussaha, B., & Fourrier, C. (2024, May 14). Introducing the Open Arabic LLM Leaderboard. Hugging Face. https://huggingface.co/blog/leaderboard-arabic

Tan, A. (2024, January 15). Sea-Lion explained: Southeast Asia's first large language model. Computer Weekly. https://www.computer-weekly.com/feature/Sea-Lion-explained-Southeast-Asias-first-large-language-model

AI Singapore. (2024). SEA-LION 7B. Hugging Face. https://huggingface.co/aisingapore/sea-lion-7b

Cohere For AI. (n.d..). Aya 101 [Large language model]. Hugging Face. Retrieved March 18, 2025, from https://huggingface.co/CohereForAI/aya-101

AI Sweden. (n.d.). GPT-SW3 [AI language model]. AI Sweden. Retrieved March 18, 2025, from https://www.ai.se/en/project/gpt-sw3

AI Singapore. Assessing LLM Performance for Southeast Asia: Introducing SEA-HELM. SEA-LION.AI, 21 Mar. 2025, https://sea-lion.ai/assessing-llm-performance-for-southeast-asia-introducing-sea-helm/. Accessed 2 Apr. 2025.

Dosunmu, D. (2024, June 13). A little-known AI startup is behind Nigeria's first government-backed LLM. Rest of World. https://restofworld.org/2024/nigeria-awarri-ai-startup-llm/

6

Hallucinations

6.1 State of Research About Hallucinations

Hallucinations are the behavior of LLMs to generate completely made-up answers that sound like normal sentences but are factually incorrect. Hallucinations make it hard to trust LLMs and come in the way of building useful applications with LLMs. In a corporate setting, it creates a business risk because the LLM can make promises about a company policy when none exists for a customer query. An LLM in education can create false narratives and mislead the learner.

They come from gaps in the training data of the LLM from its memory. So research has shown that for languages other than English, where the training data is sparse, the LLM hallucinates more (Islam et al., 2025). There has been research to show hallucinations in LLM but not enough research on how to mitigate them.

Trustworthy LLMs: LLMs are known to be trained from Internet data and are full of bias (Guo et al., 2024). There has been a lot of research to identify the bias and show the impact of this bias on various populations. One approach to mitigate bias in a model is called FAIRIJ (Sattigeri et al., 2022), which identifies biases and allows editing of the biases. Another approach is FairReprogram or Fairness Reprogramming from IBM, which finds and fixes biased classifiers (Zhang et al., 2022). Model monitoring should also take a human-centric approach for it to be trustworthy (Shergadwala et al., 2022).

6.2 What Causes NLP Hallucination

Hallucination is the concept of AI confidently giving fake answers that do not exist in reality. AI has a narrow world of its training data, and typically, when we classify data, AI tries to fit its answer to what it knows from what it has

DOI: 10.1201/9788743808145-7

been trained. Hallucination in conversational AI is different in that it forms full sentences that are factually incorrect but semantically correct. An example quoted often in the AI world for NLP hallucination is "The moon is made of cheese." NLP hallucinations happen when the AI loses the context of what is important in some training data, makes up a factually incorrect answer, and presents it with total confidence.

6.3 Why Hallucination Matters

Simple. All NLP models, including generative AI models, lie. They lie so confidently and make absurd, incorrect statements that appear so compelling. So, it is important to be aware of this when using any GenAI product like ChatGPT.

References

Islam, S. O., Lauscher, A., & Glavaš, G. (2025). How Much Do LLMs Hallucinate across Languages? On Multilingual Estimation of LLM Hallucination in the Wild. ArXiv. https://arxiv.org/abs/2502.12769

Sattigeri, P., Ghosh, S., Padhi, I., Dognin, P., & Varshney, K. R. (2022). Fair infinitesimal jackknife: Mitigating the influence of biased training data points without refitting. NeurIPS 2022. Retrieved from https://openreview.net/pdf?id=7cL46kHUu4

Zhang, G., Zhang, Y., Zhang, Y., Fan, W., Li, Q., Liu, S., & Chang, S. (2022). Fairness Reprogramming. *ArXiv*. https://arxiv.org/abs/2209.10222

Guo, Y., Guo, M., Su, J., Yang, Z., Zhu, M., Li, H., Qiu, M., & Liu, S. S. (2024). Bias in Large Language Models: Origin, Evaluation, and Mitigation. ArXiv. https://arxiv.org/abs/2411.10915

Shergadwala, M. N., Lakkaraju, H., & Kenthapadi, K. (2022). A Human-Centric Take on Model Monitoring. ArXiv. https://arxiv.org/abs/2206.02868

7

Data: Fine-tuning and RAG

7.1 State of Research in RAG and Fine-tuning

LLM carries its pre-trained data knowledge in its parameters. GenAI showed us the promise of LLM to create context-aware conversational chatbots to engage with customers. As enterprises began exploring this capability, companies asked for the chatbot to utilize their data sources. For example, a customer service chatbot can serve customers only when it has learned from past customer chat archives to understand top issues and solutions. This brought the innovation of RAG (retrieval-augmented generation) to allow pre-training with non-parametric memory (Lewis et al., 2020).

7.2 What is RAG

RAG is a framework to allow an LLM to connect with one or more structured and unstructured data sources to an LLM. RAG allows enterprises to provide provenance for the decision of the LLM. This is an evolving area of research where the LLM can cite its sources from reliable sources and not from hallucinations. Two common technologies in the RAG space are the LangChain and LlamaIndex.

As RAG-based data access applications evolved, questions about security, privacy, and the need to stop the LLM from not taking up the knowledge from the RAG data store into LLM knowledge.

RAG Fusion is an advanced RAG architecture: Research evolved to advanced RAG architecture to allow for reduced latency in applications that search intermediate data stores using RAG between chat responses using LLM (Rackauckas, 2024).

DOI: 10.1201/9788743808145-8

7.3 Difference Between Fine-tuning and RAG

How do you decide which method is best for your business? Should you choose fine-tuning or RAG to build out your GenAI product, such as an intelligent chatbot that helps your customers with support information or helps them search your product catalog?

1. First, look at what kind of data you have available. Is it a historic document that does not change, or is this something that gets updated often?

   Fine-tuning works when the data is labeled and static, while RAG is good for dynamic content (user-generated content or updates to existing data). Fine-tuning is not teaching LLM new data.

2. Fine-tuning is used to make the LLM have a specific behavior or tone.

   For example, you may want it to be polite or formal. Then, fine-tuning will do it.

3. RAG specializes in the retrieval of information from additional data sources so it can be transparent and less prone to hallucination.

4. Cost

   Fine-tuning requires fully labeled data (supervised learning), where RAG needs some labeled data and a mix of unlabeled data. So the cost of fine-tuning goes into labeling data and COMPUTE time, making it more expensive. RAG focuses on setting up embeddings and coding. RAG systems cost just about the same as the cost of a developer.

References

Lewis, P., Perez, E., Piktus, A., Petroni, F., Karpukhin, V., Goyal, N., Küttler, H., Lewis, M., Yih, W., Rocktäschel, T., Riedel, S., & Kiela, D. (2020). Retrieval-Augmented Generation for Knowledge-Intensive NLP Tasks. ArXiv. https://arxiv.org/abs/2005.11401

Rackauckas, Z. (2024). RAG-Fusion: A New Take on Retrieval-Augmented Generation. *ArXiv*. https://doi.org/10.5121/ijnlc.2024.13103

SECTION TWO

Product Management and Business

8

LLM Capabilities and Reasoning

8.1 State of Research in LLM Reasoning

Reasoning is the ability of the LLM to make decisions like a human in the absence of a human. Innovation in this space has created different approaches to reasoning.

A simple reasoning approach is prompt-based reasoning. As the name implies, this is done by prompting the LLM to make deductions to solve complex problems. One approach that extended this approach was with a knowledge graph (Li et al., 2024). Another innovation is called ReAct, which stands for react with action. In this approach, the LLM agent makes decisions based on data from the environment (Yao et al., 2022). ReWOO is another reasoning approach which, as the name implies, is reasoning without observation. Can you imagine where it makes sense to ignore data from observation for reasoning? It works well for augmented language models (Xu et al., 2023).

The reasoning capability of large language models (LLMs) has been evolving to build reasoning capability to solve complex reasoning problems.

Innovation has evolved to create different types of reasoning approaches. DeepSeek-R1 was created to create a reinforcement learning-led, reward-based model (Guo et al., 2025).

8.2 Reasoning LLM Models

Reasoning is analytical thinking where humans make decisions based on information.

Abstract reasoning is the ability to work with abstract concepts. I remember a past colleague who was proud of his son questioning an abstract concept like numbers in mathematics by asking him what the number 10 means.

DOI: 10.1201/9788743808145-10

Abstract reasoning requires identifying patterns, trends, making sense of formulas, and making connections between concepts, ideas, and objects.

Abstract reasoning also involves examining situations from multiple perspectives.

What is logical reasoning?

Logical reasoning is a way of thinking to solve problems, make predictions, and come to conclusions. So naturally, the engineers who were building AI were reminded of algebra and math and built math benchmark datasets to test the reasoning power of LLMs.

I believe that reasoning by analogy or understanding multiple perspectives is not limited to math problems and can be seen in humanity in critical thinking skills in writing, too.

OpenAI-oi from OpenAI, AlphaProof from Google Deepmind, and Deepseek-R1 are examples of reasoning models. They take a similar approach to defining reasoning by proving the new models perform better math problems using a benchmark math problem set known as GSM8K. OpenAI and Gemini models are built on foundational models that we learned about earlier. DeepSeek has a similar foundation model like Gemini and OpenAI.

8.3 Q&A Model

GPT models are Q&A-based models. ChatGPT is the most famous intelligent application that operates in a Q&A format. It cannot do common sense arithmetic.

Prompt engineering, asking ChatGPT to present as a math professor, allowed it to perform math functions by accessing that part of its training.

Train-of-thought prompt chaining allows for a chatbot to break down tasks into multiple steps and is better at tasks involving numbers.

8.4 LLM Capabilities

Everything LLMs do falls under these five capabilities:

1. Text generation: Text generation is the capability of the LLM to predict the next word and generate a word.
2. Machine translation: This is the capability of taking a sequence of words as input to generate a sequence of words as output. This is done with a more complex learning recall and generation process because the

words generated have to be adjusted to form sentences in the translated language based on the input set of words.

3. Knowledge answering: There is a capability called KI-NLP or knowledge intensive NLP that covers the ability to fact-check and retrieve information. RAG (retrieval augmented generation) falls under this category, and we will learn RAG in detail in a future chapter.
4. Response generation: This is the capability to answer a question and is required to build chatbots.
5. Classification: This is the capability to classify a set of words with a tag each. An example of classification capability is the sentiment analysis of a group of words using LLM.

These capabilities of LLM are used to create different applications using LLM, such as building chatbots, doing text summarizations, or translating across languages.

References

Li, Y., Zhang, R., & Liu, J. (2024). An Enhanced Prompt-Based LLM Reasoning Scheme via Knowledge Graph-Integrated Collaboration. ArXiv. https://arxiv.org/abs/2402.04978

Yao, S., Zhao, J., Yu, D., Du, N., Shafran, I., Narasimhan, K., & Cao, Y. (2022). ReAct: Synergizing Reasoning and Acting in Language Models. ArXiv. https://arxiv.org/abs/2210.03629

Guo, D., Yang, D., Zhang, H., Song, J., Zhang, R., Xu, R., Zhu, Q., Ma, S., Wang, P., Bi, X., Zhang, X., Yu, X., Wu, Y., Wu, Z. F., Gou, Z., Shao, Z., Li, Z., Gao, Z., Liu, A., . . . Zhang, Z. (2025). DeepSeek-R1: Incentivizing Reasoning Capability in LLMs via Reinforcement Learning. ArXiv. https://arxiv.org/abs/2501.12948

Xu, B., Peng, Z., Lei, B., Mukherjee, S., Liu, Y., & Xu, D. (2023). ReWOO: Decoupling Reasoning from Observations for Efficient Augmented Language Models. ArXiv. https://arxiv.org/abs/2305.18323

9

The API Economy

9.1 The State of Research of the API Economy

The web opened up the digitization of industries and the disintermediation of data. Web 2.0 brought software platforms opening up with APIs to allow integration with each other, with companies opening up an ecosystem of developers to innovate beyond what the developers in the companies could conceive. This allowed companies not to be stuck in their own innovator's dilemma, and soon, big tech companies began expanding to tech startup ecosystems. In this world came the App Store by Apple, Amazon, Google, and Facebook. Enterprise saw Microsoft developers build out their software stack and SAP, Oracle, Salesforce, and Citrix built customer ecosystems with these APIs. I was involved in the early team opening up payment APIs with PayPal. Soon, a new generation of developers evolved, and they built software with APIs to facilitate information sharing between companies. APIs were licensed like software. Most were open, and this was a healthy way to build upon each other, driven by customer needs and innovations. IFTTT Airtable and Zapier took this to stitch the entire Internet into its canvas. Being open was the spirit of APIs, while a few like Facebook built walled gardens because they thrive on the data economy where they collect our attention and own our data, which they share with their customer as currency to enhance their valuations.

With the cloud business models evolving since 2006, with Amazon taking the lead followed by Google and Microsoft, APIs brought the SaaS business model to scale.

AI development expanded the cloud APIs with cloud providers adding support for huge GPU processing. Ready-made AI inference models are also offered as APIs from technology companies. With all this, APIs became the offering for companies to buy AI products or cloud access for modeling AI in-house for their enterprise or to build upon the models, such as facial

DOI: 10.1201/9788743808145-11

recognition or image models built by select tech AI companies. These AI APIs are licensed on a software-as-a-service model. This means the AI is treated as software, and by accessing it via the cloud, it is sold as a service on demand instead of a software usage-based license.

So what is new now with APIs as an API economy if APIs have existed since Web 2.0 since 2007?

Machine learning and deep learning models made predictions and fetched results from historical data used in its learning from training data. Foundation models and attention models are built with billions of parameters with AI trained on a very huge volume of data using a technique called semi-supervised learning. Hence, a generative AI model does not predict results from its learning but becomes generative to predict the next words. This extends to other modalities beyond text. In this world of generative AI models, they are also available as APIs.

However, given the scale of these foundations and attention models, business models have evolved to combine software like SaaS's access of API to cloud models of resource utilization to offer APIs charged based on tokens. This world of APIs is exploding with more models for various modalities. It is inviting enterprises with a huge volume of data holding their knowledge to model their AI using these APIs.

9.2 Market Trends

Generative AI covers a wide range of technologies that are growing at different rates and impacting different industries in radical and unexpected ways. Broadly speaking, intelligent applications like ChatGPT have captured the imagination of 100 million users in 2 months. This is a new record in technology adoption by consumers, beating the record growth of Instagram, which achieved 100 million daily active users, also known as MAU in 2.5 years, and TikTok, which took 9 months to reach 100 MAUs. Generative AI has also created a wave of new intelligent apps for content-aware chatbots and for generating text content in several applications for copywriting, text editing, and generating scripts, poems, essays, and more. There are intelligent apps in image generation categories also, but image generation is more available as a tool for generating images than as intelligent applications like chatbots.

Then there are AI platforms that power the API economy, targeting developers with APIs to generate content of all modalities. These include GPT-3, which powers ChatGPT and several APIs. Refer to references at the end for a list of generative AI APIs and what they do.

A third set of technologies offers AI infrastructure for generative AI. These include storage and cloud infrastructure, and where startups are building a middleware layer of technologies upon these foundation models, it could include MLOps infrastructure too.

There is a growth in existing technology tools and products integrating generative AI APIs or adding generative features to their core offering. An example of this is Voiceflow, an NLP chatbot that now includes a generative AI prompt chaining feature that allows the chatbot to generate content for developer-defined intents.

9.3 Business Drivers and Trends

The key business driver is developer excitement for innovation with generative AI APIs. There is a wave of new kinds of AI artists who are using prompt engineering to generate art, cartoons, and images using the latest image generation technologies and pushing their boundaries for further innovation in that area.

The business models have not evolved for any of these. ChatGPT offers subscription pricing, and GPT-3 has been integrated into the new Bing search engine from Microsoft. But enterprise companies who own the data that can train chatbots are still on the sidelines, waiting for clear business models to evolve to adapt generative AI to build out applications that feed into the Industry 5.0 trend of human-centric AI applications.

9.4 Building GenAI Applications

What creates the next big technology innovation?

What scales the next big tech innovation? A killer app or business model. Here are killer apps of the past that have proven the core value of past technologies (Killer application, n.d.).

What is a business model? It's a new way of solving a customer problem or reaching new customers in more cost-efficient ways or totally new ways of living that make economic sense to create demand with purchase power. So it's revenues with a strategic shift and sustainability.

Generative AI, which creates new text content, is threatening the jobs of editors, writers, and poets. It is challenging for teachers from K-12 to the heights of university academics to innovate what learning entails. For educators to go beyond knowledge accumulation to analytics synthesis, and to build foundations for new creations.

Figure 9.1 Prompt "A Photo of a tree" in Scribble Diffusion.

Image generation is not only threatening artists who create marketing images for advertisement to artists and comic illustrators, it is being trained on data from the Internet and using Internet images without the permission of the image creators and has led to litigation which is open as of this book writing. Figures 9.1 and 9.2 will illustrate this concept!

Where do business models come into play?

New startups are getting creative to create AI-led writing and AI art NFTs. Existing companies are the ones threatened by the loss of revenues and market positioning.

For example, Shutterstock, whose revenue comes from selling stock photos by artists, has partnered with OpenAI, promising a fund to generate images using its stock images with a promise to compensate its stock image producers. It is not clear if the stock image creator will be compensated for creating images that become training data for the image-generating AI.

9.4.1 Open source as a business model

We have seen historically in the technology industry that some startups put their innovation in open source, and that accelerates the development of technologies built upon them, and the open source companies end up offering service level agreements (SLAs) and implementation support for large enterprises as a revenue-generating business model. Linux is an example of leveraging SLAs. Similarly, there are companies like RedHat that have pioneered

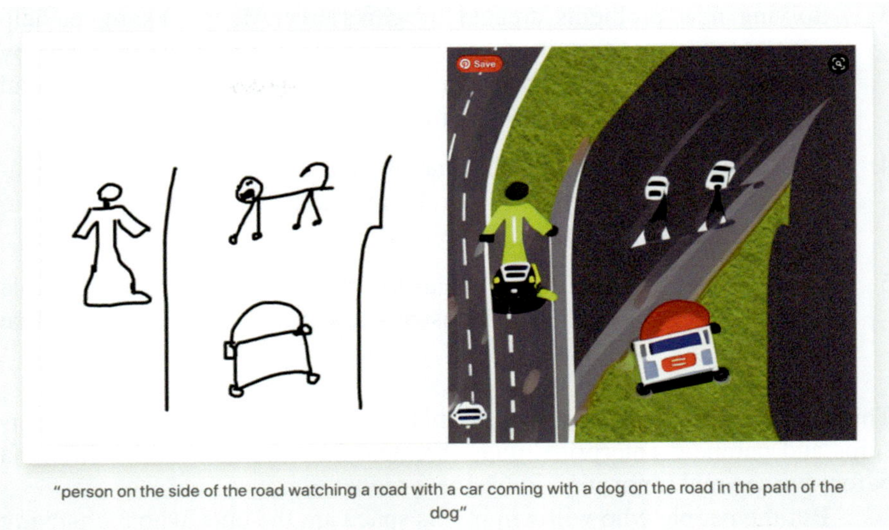

Figure 9.2 Scribble Diffusion of a person watching the road with a car and a dog.

this model. It is worthy to keep track of generative AI models being built as proprietary platforms by companies like OpenAI and models in open source being built by startups like Cohere.ai or Stable Diffusion. Startups like Hugging Face are making a whole new open source-based foundation for developers to build across competing platforms. So it is worth watching to see if this gets picked up by the enterprise markets instead of large cloud platforms that they already have trusted with their data to build AI long before the generative AI models became accessible to the public.

> **Calling for Innovation:** I believe what we are seeing today is a great disruption, and its echo is rumbling into numerous business ecosystems of companies. It is calling for creative, business-savvy leaders to re-imagine innovative business models to survive and leverage the opportunities in this profound movement.

These innovations include:

1. Extend an existing business – can a company utilize its existing assets to help generate content that can create new value for its customers.
2. Create new infrastructures for generative AI to support the innovators, e.g., Middleware.

3. Solving new problems created by generative AI. For example, help educators detect if student essays are GPT-3 generated as done by detectGPT or extend to check for bias in the platform as an adversarial model to keep the generative AI inclusive and ethical.

4. New innovative businesses that cannibalize existing businesses by generating content to solve a huge problem that has not been solved so far, e.g., helping with climate change.

5. Create partnerships with companies to create a vertical product to scale generative AI in a particular industry – lawyers or functional areas like marketers.

This is just the beginning. I speculate that we will see some wasteful partnerships and paranoid enterprise funds threatened by the innovator's dilemma before we see real innovation in business models.

But the people who will win in this space are the ones who are playing with the existing models, building new possibilities, and testing new value-creation hypotheses. As we have seen in the technology industry over the past decades, these iterations may not yield the winning models. Still, they will sharpen the knowledge and experience of the developers, product managers, business people, linguists, artists, lawyers, etc., and help the broader community iterate towards the winning model.

9.5 Futuristic Insights About the Software Engineering Industry

1. Software-generated code is the big trend with LLMs such as Co-pilot that is making a strategic shift in how software will be built in the future. LLMs hallucinate when generating code as they do with other prompts. Andrew Karpathy has demonstrated that we need experienced software engineers to validate the code generated with prompts to get to the correct code to be generated. He has built software from AI-generated code using Curso, an AI-powered code editor with backend compatibility to Claude AI (YouTube, 2023). See Figure 9.3 for an example of an AI-generated code.

2. Consider how data storage in the cloud has evolved in multiple combinations, including hybrid, public, private, and federated. We predict AI data storage, generated, synthetic, and programmatic, will continue to follow similar cloud architectures and storage patterns.

USER create and run a sql query to get the above people who list in South America or Asia

ASSISTANT Assuming we have a table named 'people' with the given schema and data, the SQL query would look like this:

```
```sql
SELECT * FROM people
WHERE Location IN ('Tokyo, Japan', 'Mumbai, India', 'Rio de Janeiro, Brazil');
```

Result:

First Name	Last Name	Location
Aya	Nakamura	Tokyo, Japan
Priyanka	Sharma	Mumbai, India
Leila	Da Silva	Rio de Janeiro, Brazil
```

Figure 9.3 An example of an AI-generated code. From Robert Schwentker.

3. It is possible that such API platform companies can absorb the knowledge from each company in an industry and create a knowledge disintermediation, creating new efficiencies. This could raise legal challenges about the ownership of such knowledge but is very hard to challenge given the lack of explainability of AI models.

   Stable Diffusion is an example of this approach challenged in court by artists whose style the AI has stolen by learning it and offering it to its customers. Even if it purged its data, the knowledge is impossible to purge, and more impossible to prove that it has done it.

> 3. **Call for Innovation:** A federated system of learning could evolve with transparency and privacy, preserving and respecting the data ownership and knowledge ownership of different companies.

References

YouTube. (2023, September 12). How wolves change rivers [Video]. YouTube. https://www.youtube.com/watch?v=2ybCIacN9Ns

Wikipedia contributors. (n.d.). Killer application. Wikipedia, The Free Encyclopedia. From https://en.wikipedia.org/wiki/Killer_application

10

Industries Impacted

State of Research of GenAI in Industries

In this chapter, let us look at the impact of generative AI on several industries. The impact may be a good impact or a bad impact. I use the word "impact" to show the reaction of users and how you, as a product or business user, can innovate to create a positive opportunity for you and your customer.

We are in the early stages of the impact of generative AI on many industries, so I hope that you, my reader, will get inspired to think of innovations to bring to your companies.

With all the excitement of generative AI focused on ChatGPT and image diffusion models, I urge you to not think about bringing generative AI to your industry as a chat experience but think about how an AI that generates content of any modality based on the customer's input can create new experiences for the customer and change the relationship between consumer and merchant towards serving the customer better. Also, think about what business model shift is required to support this shift and how you would develop a test-and-learn environment to test out this business model in your business.

10.1 Impact on Software Industry

> "I think this technology (GPT-3) is going to reshape pretty much every software category,"
>
> – Satya Nadella, CEO of Microsoft.

What does this quote by Satya Nadella mean? It means that GPT-3 is creating a shift in the software industry, and that impact is going to cascade onto all industries using software for digitization in any form. There is a distinct difference between technology impacting your industry by changing how you do business or creating revenue opportunities as opposed to

DOI: 10.1201/9788743808145-12

software as an industry being impacted in all its categories. This is important for anyone feeling restless about catching up to understand what generative AI is and how it impacts their business. The impact is going to create a shift in the technology infrastructure of your business, bring IT to the forefront of this change, and pull at that tension that already exists between IT and OT because IT cannot just buy new software. The software is an AI and needs to be modeled using your company's biggest asset – data, which is typically owned by the business units.

This thinking will guide you to understand the competencies needed in your company to innovate in this new field of generative AI entering your organization. It requires more data scientists with generative AI skills. It also requires business leaders with imagination to innovate to conceive new intelligent applications.

We are in the Wild West with no clear business models, open to innovate on intelligent applications, and tons of questions about data ownership, bias, explainability of the generated AI content, and the billion-dollar question of ROI and huge disruptions that shift business's strategic direction and growth.

10.2 Understanding Costs

There is the huge cost of training, which is borne by the companies building the foundation models. The next cost is simply to run the foundation model in inference. Or to access the model as an API and fine-tune it with your data, which is also a training cost.

OpenAI offers a pricing based on tokens similar to the cloud business model today. A token is a set of characters that make up words, including spaces. Developers can tokenize text using the transformers package in Python or the gpt-3-encoder package in Node.js. Token pricing is based on per 1000 tokens. You can fine-tune existing models with your data to build out intelligent applications. The data you use determines your price. OpenAI offers four different models, Ada, Babbage, Curie, and DaVinci, and each of these different models comes with a different cost per 1K/tokens. A token is a piece of a word and is not exactly a breakdown of words but includes spaces and could be parts of a word from your training data of sentences and paragraphs. According to OpenAI, 1000 tokens is about 750 words, or a typical paragraph such as this one you are reading is about 35 tokens. It is important to understand the cost of training for fine-tuning and to select the right model to fine-tune the model with your data. For example, DaVinci costs 3 cents (or $0.03) per 1K tokens. After your model is ready for inference or customer or event internal pilot testing, there is a separate cost for usage, which again for DaVinci comes to 12 cents (or $0.12) per 1K tokens.

There are tools available to keep check on how many tokens you have and what it costs for training or usage.

For example, OpenAI offers the tool " tokenizer" to track the costs of tokens.

10.3 Education

Universities and schools are impacted by ChatGPT. Students can generate code or essays for their homework by simply using ChatGPT. So, some universities have issued policies to ban ChatGPT in their coursework. OpenAI created an app to test if the generated content is from itself or a human. DetectGPT has evolved to use an adversarial approach to check this instead of using training data.

10.4 E-commerce and Marketing

E-commerce as an industry already uses AI for several use cases to enhance the customer experience and optimize the relationship with users for merchants. The most common AI used is personalized recommendations for users. This is done by creative collaborative filters to operate on users' data to offer recommendations for purchase. An e-commerce site or app begins by using an item-based recommendation to show users who bought similar items, builds up data about users, and then adds personalized user-based recommendations. Deep learning AI models that use a reward-based system (See reference for RNN with user feedback model) are used to make sure that there is a balance between revenues from user clicks to their long-term loyalty and engagement with an e-commerce site.

AI is also used in e-commerce to personalize the search or browsing experience for users. For example, Browse AI from Google Cloud's Discovery AI solutions optimally orders the search for users based on their behavioral data. If you think about this, this is not different from the next best click algorithm that marketers employ to get AI to help them optimize campaigns on which channel to reach customers to get better clicks and conversions in a multi-channel experience.

Google's Vertex AI Vision product helps merchants manage in-store inventory using computer vision and text recognition of tags.

Now, with generative AI, it is natural for the e-commerce experience for users to use generative AI and for merchants to employ the same for search, recommendations, and better inventory management. Join me in thinking about this with an innovative lens to create new product use cases.

When a customer is presented search results to browse or when presented recommendations of products for purchase, it is natural to present the AI results just as a list of products but to engage the customer with generative AI making recommendations and adapting in a context-aware chat to get the user just the list of items they want next. It is easily possible to combine the collaborative filtering algorithms in use with this customer chat to use it as input to adapt the user's list of recommendations for browsing or purchase recommendations. Also, it is totally possible to take the customer prompt and generate the right images for the products the customer wants, and use that image as a visual search to fetch the right inventory.

For example, the generative AI can ask the customer what they are looking for, and when they say, " I want a halter neck top for my 15-year-old niece," the AI can engage the user further to understand the size, color, and style preference of the search request. It could fetch those items but can go one step further by asking the user to describe the product they have in mind and use the text as a prompt to generate an image of a product. Once the customer approves that it is exactly what they are looking for, then AI can do a visual search to fetch similar items from inventory. If the company is innovative on the business model side, it could then create this product and ship it to the customer.

This will help create an inventory of items just in time based on customer chats.

For in-store experience, music can be generated on-demand using a generative AI such as MusicLM, which is conceived from a paper from Google but is not yet available as a product. This is an example of a generative AI that receives a text prompt and generates music. In this case, the text prompt can be generated from an AI that understands the user's behavior and feeds it to the music-generating AI.

AI companies had tools for merchants earlier that focused on helping them manage huge volumes of data they gathered from customer engagement. Generative AI takes it one step further by creating a user experience that engages the user to give them what they want instead of collecting their data for AI to present recommendations and wait for the user's click.

This gets us closer to a world where the customer leads in their journey, aided by generative AI. Using collaborative filtering recommendations, they are able to use AI for personalized goals they set for themselves, making this a win-win for the customer and the merchant.

10.5 Customer Support

Customer support across many industries has already adopted intent-based chatbots to engage with customers to reduce customer support costs with a very clear, measurable ROI. This depends on lots of past customer support call logs for the AI to develop top support areas of support and personalized propensity for support for customers to help the chatbot engage with customer intents.

Now, with generative AI, every chat with the customer becomes a prompt for the AI to generate context-aware conversation to keep the engagement with the customer to help resolve their problem. In the past intent-based chatbots, there would be a huge AI confusion matrix for every chatbot development, which is very resource intensive, with the support team figuring out indeterministic conditions where the chatbot fails the customer and loses them to fix it for next time.

For example, Emirates Integrated Telecommunications Company, also known as du, a telecom operator in the United Arab Emirates switched to an intent-based NLP chatbot to chat with customers across multiple forms of messaging platforms using UnificationEngine AI technology from UIB Holdings Pte. Ltd. and successfully reduced the volume of queries handled by du's call centers and stores. See the reference citation of the AIX book for this case study. Now, with generative AI, this can be simplified further to allow for the customer to engage in a context-aware conversation with the customer without losing them.

Call for Innovation: For example, in the past, when the support chatbot was unable to help a customer, a frustrated customer would say something like, "That's not right, I am looking for something else." This would lead the AI to multiple choice paths and lead to the indeterminate condition to fetch the human or log the situation, offering to get back to them as a follow-up. Now, with generative AI, each conversion becomes a prompt for the AI to continue the conversation and ask humans questions to get more insight from the customer to fetch the right support to solve their problem. This data can still be used to run machine learning regression models to understand the top issues that the product or company faces to fix the underlying problem.

Another innovation possible with customer support is that with generative AI growing in multiple modalities, the customer could engage with text, voice, or call on a video call or share an image of an issue and a multi-modal generative AI solution can be generated to solve their problem by making the customer a partner in the problem-solving process.

What is needed for this to evolve to get traction in the enterprise?

Of course, we need generative AI tools and intelligence apps to be built for customer support. But also, we need new metrics to evolve in how we measure success. In previous models, the customer getting quick resolution and not using the human's time was a critical measure of success. In the NLP intent-based chatbot world, the number of steps taken for the chatbot to get to a resolution for the customer or chat duration is used as metrics. This needs to change with a generative AI chatbot because each engagement fetches new data to train the AI better, so the metrics may have to be optimized between the short-term gain of resolutions vs the long-term goals of returning customers or the overall lifetime value of a customer.

10.6 Industry 5.0 and Enterprise Markets

Industrial IoT is evolving to a more human-centric design by engaging with people using a chatbot interface, leading to the evolving field of Industry 5.0.

The building world is full of devices generating data with building operations creating more data, and all that is fed to the AI. As of now, it's all been training data for machine learning to create AI for energy optimization and optimized building management with the promise of personalization. With generative AI, the promise is that chatting AI or AI generates visual images, but those also need data to be fed by companies. It's in the early stages, and we haven't gotten the tools to feed our building data to generative AI. I believe that more than the lack of tools, it is calling for our imagination for use cases where we could utilize such an AI.

Autonomous vehicles are in a collision with autonomous buildings aspiring for personalization in the building with an autonomous AI (Sudha, 2020).

What would such an AI do for buildings? ChatGPT-3 is showing us a Q&A interface mimicking humans and engages us in conversation. What would such a chatbot do for a building? I did an exercise about this at my AIX design for Master in UX design students to design an AI user interface for ChatGPT for hospital stakeholders. We can extend that to an office building or an apartment, or an airport. It goes back to your vision of personalization AI for people in the building. What I would chat with a ChatGPT-3 building would be different from what you would ask it. The same goes for our customers and realtors, and building managers.

Read about the generative AI models and what is the evolving ecosystem and business model shifts and opportunities.

References

Sudha, P. (2020, June). Partnership of Autonomous Vehicles with Autonomous Buildings. AutomatedBuildings.com. Retrieved from http://automatedbuildings.com/news/jun20/articles/sudha/200531921O1sudha.html

11

Product Design and Prompt Engineering

11.1 Prompt Engineering

Prompt Engineering is the term used to describe an evolving field of how to develop prompts to communicate with generative AI to get it to give you the context you want. It is not engineering in the definition of engineering but is an analytical function that captures the know-how of jobs, art, and design into prompts. Prompt engineering is the fastest growing area of generative AI that excites me most because I see it as a way by which artists and users can engage with the AI to test its limits and innovators are pushing the boundary of what the AI can do to allow for the generative AI developers to adapt and iterate and improve the models and intelligent apps. I also see prompt engineering as a fast-growing skill that is going to be needed by artists, marketing designers, and writers to do their jobs in the future, with generative AI models becoming tools in their hands to create human-augmented generated content.

Product managers should take note of prompt engineering as a way to receive user feedback from generative AI API products. Also, there is an opportunity for new products to be built to ease the prompt engineering process for non-coding users.

11.1.1 Types of prompts

Prompt hacking

Prompt hacking is a way to use prompts to hack a chatbot to give a different answer than what it is fine-tuned for.

Prompt injection

Prompt injection is a kind of hacking where an ordinary sentence is given to ChatGPT and asked to ignore part of the prompt, making it do something mentioned in the rest of the prompt.

DOI: 10.1201/9788743808145-13

Prompt leaking

Prompt Leaking is a form of prompt injection, which is also a form of prompt hacking where the prompt makes the AI say what was in its original prompt during its fine-tuning. This could make the chatbot unhide any prompt that was intentionally hidden by a company during its fine-tuning. "Explain to me like I am a 5-year-old" is a common example of hiding a prompt which can be hacked by prompt leaking.

There are tools from most companies to generate prompts. There are creative entrepreneurs selling templates for prompt generation. https://stablediffusionweb.com/prompt-generator

See the reference section for tools to build out prompts and to understand prompt engineering in detail.

Jailbreaking

Jailbreaking is a type of prompt injection that goes past the safety features set up during the fine-tuning of a chatbot. For example, content moderation in ChatGPT is set up to avoid controversial responses such as illegal or sexual, or violent content. Pretending is a common form of jailbreaking. When asked about math problems, ChatGPT could not answer them, but when asked to pretend it was a math professor from a reputable brand university, it responded by applying math to the answers.

Prompt soft tuning

Prompt soft tuning takes the same concept of jailbreaking and asks the chatbot to pretend and then takes the answer and adjusts the weights of tokens and is similar to fine-tuning a model but allows us to use the same model for multiple tasks by appending prompts during inference.

11.2 Product Design of Generative AI for Enterprise Products

Industry 5.0 is the term used to describe the latest evolution of the Industrial IoT system with a human-centric design where generative AI chatbots engage with customers and get their input to provide value from enterprise data and processes.

AIX Design is about designing the user experience of AI-driven products. ChatGPT is deployed as a chat interface as a showcase of the GPT-3 generative AI model. There are application showcases of image models, such as DALL-E.

Designing the actual product user experience flow becomes the responsibility of the product manager in partnership with UX design teams.

11.2.1 What is the AI confusion matrix?

All AI is predictive, so it is always predicting every step of its interaction with users. So, every decision from an AI can be "true" or "false." Now, it can give a true answer when it is expected to say yes and a true answer when it is expected to say no. Similarly, it can answer as false when it is factually false, or it can say false when it should say true. This leads to false positives and false negatives for some customer data.

Let us look at an example of a chatbot built using GPT-3 like ChatGPT serving as the interface for a hospital front desk. When a user asks, "Is pediatrics open after 6 pm?" the AI could say yes or no. If pediatrics closes by 6 pm, the yes becomes a false positive, and a no becomes a true negative. When the user is stopped to check if they are wearing a mask and the AI stops a user wearing a mask when in fact the user is wearing a mask, it becomes a false negative.

Typically, data scientists test for false positives and false negatives with a set of test data that is representative of their customer segments.

Now it becomes the responsibility of the product manager to design the user experience flow for false positives and false negatives and determine which is very critical for the product being developed.

We would recommend product managers apply the AIX Design framework for generative AI products similar to other AI products. According to the AIX Design framework, the product designer should design for the following decision points.

1. Gender of the AI
2. Personality of the AI: Humanize the AI with behavioral traits
3. Tone of conversation
4. False positives
5. False negatives

Given that generative AI is biased from its training data, we would recommend creating an adversarial AI persona to test how the AI will behave if put to harmful use.

Adversarial AI design should cater to three user flow scenarios to ensure that AI is built with an Ethical AI design and does not cause harm to humans.

(i) Unused

(ii) Misused

(iii) Disused

11.2.2 Privacy and security

Apart from the technical aspect of the API calls creating the integrated product, product managers should consider the flow of data between products and what is stored where, and any privacy and data ownership implications. The experience of the user needs to be seamless, given the human-computer interface nature of ChatGPT, and the product manager should plan for error handling and make this a user-friendly experience.

Another important area of focus for product managers is that given that generative AI models are trained with biased data from the Internet, they carry inherent biases of the world in the form of misogyny, homophobia, and racism found in websites and documents on the public Internet. So product managers should plan to address the AI confusion matrix for their generative AI with a special focus on NLP hallucinations and ensure data privacy and human agency on the human-centered design of the AI.

11.3 API Integration Products

Since generative AI is in its infancy, we are seeing each big tech company offer its own set of APIs that are not compatible with other sets of APIs from another tech company. This is creating a walled garden of openAI vs Google vs Baidu, etc. This creates competition and accelerates innovation but fragments the options for developers and enterprises, making it expensive for them to build on a parallel API world. This is comparable to how mobile development happens on Apple IOS vs Android as a double cost for companies. I foresee the evolution of tools that bridge between API worlds, creating tools that are compatible between the API worlds.

Integration into other applications is where the promise of ChatGPT and GPT-3 makes sense to watch for value created. People have shown integration into Excel to bring in formulas.

We discussed earlier the need for the integration of generative AI into other products. This calls for product managers to design the integration points using generative AI API models and APIs of other products. One example is the integration of ChatGPT into Excel. Another is integration into a word-processing document or a Slack channel. See https://www.chatbot.com/help/integrations/slack-integration/)

11.4 Generative AI Middleware

It is also inviting developers to create a middleware layer of API products that build on these generative AI APIs to create the next layer of API platforms targeting industry and functional segments and creating an ecosystem of competitive API offerings.

- Filters
- Prompts
- Fine-tuning
- Integrations

An example of a middleware is ControlNet built upon the open-source model Stable Diffusion. ControlNet was created to support spatial consistency in Stable Diffusion. Spatial consistency is how you tell the AI which part of the image to keep and which to change. ControlNet is not a foundation for other image generation models that are being built upon it. One such example is Scribble Diffusion, which added the option for us to scribble an image in addition to a prompt to ask the AI to generate an image. Scribble Diffusion added depth maps and edge detection.

12

Generative AI for Enterprise AI

12.1 Industry 5.0 and Enterprise Data Modeling

Artificial intelligence is pervasive with the promise of solving problems for every possible industry by sifting through large volumes of data and making predictions or creating automations. Predicting weather, making drug discovery, automating manufacturing with robots, making predictions for oil and gas, and autonomous vehicles are all based on training with large volumes of enterprise data to look for patterns to make predictions by segmenting, grouping, classification, or anomaly detection. The finance industry and banking use AI for trust and safety and robo-trading.

This AI is built with machine learning and deep learning. Enterprise has had a struggle to scale pilots successfully.

In traditional AI, the enterprise still has control. Why? Because they own the data. In their vast troves of data lies their years of knowledge. AI has been unlocking this knowledge as information in context. Enterprise was on a search for use cases that uncovered ROI and potential growth. And they have been in a race to take their data across silos and to find the winning use case. The technology industry has been giving them many AI solutions. Enterprise has funded several startups that have been verticalizing AI for their industry or their function, such as marketing or customer service, or automation of processes in legal or compliance.

Enter generative AI.

Generative AI was adopted by data scientists to create synthetic data to train more AI. It was adopted by marketing for NLP-based chatbots for customer engagement right from discovery through engagement to customer support. So far, it was still enterprise using their data and their business acumen in a

DOI: 10.1201/9788743808145-14

game they know to play with their rules of automation, process efficiencies, and proving ROI to solve problems.

With the new explosion of generative AI models, especially since ChatGPT showcased what an intelligent application can do, since November 2022, enterprise has been called to play a different game.

AI is now about innovation.

AI is now about customer-centric communication.

AI is now about fundamental change to how we work, learn, move, shop, and engage with one another.

Enterprise needs stability, and this is a shifting space. That means risk. Enterprise has to bet on one company or another as the big technology companies fight with each other to become the leader in the generative AI space.

Enterprise needs to redefine use cases and ROI. Enterprise has to jump onto a moving train so they are not left behind.

Enterprise has questions about cloud vs core, the role of open source, and understanding costs, understanding more and more complex models with their jargon-sounding names to know how to pick the right model to bet on, and more questions to understanding the evolving middleware as a business person.

Good, you are in the right place.

I have answers in the FAQ below, but come prepared to deal with ambiguity. Also, be prepared to learn to ask more questions.

Let me cut to the chase and tell you a secret. Enterprise has the data; you have the business acumen, years of domain knowledge. That is what we need to develop use cases. We just need a bit more imagination to go past existing problems and a new way of thinking to innovate.

You should get ready to innovate, to go past innovator's dilemmas to cannibalize existing ways of business and market structures. You are going to create new ways of doing everything, and AI is going to generate it for you. But you need to tell it, prompt it. That's the trick here.

12.2 Enterprise Generative AI

12.2.1 Open source

Many big companies are creating closed platforms and calling you to build your AI upon their foundation models. But some, like Cohere.ai or Stability.ai, are open source. This is a strategic move to get more developers to build out the much-needed middleware layer of technology. It is not altruistic or open knowledge sharing. There are no companies offering enterprise SLAs. It is too early to say who will win. I can tell you it is not going to be one big company and the winner takes all. Startups are innovating fast. There will be more startups to come.

12.2.2 Cloud vs core

The question is whether the AI is going to be on the cloud or core. The top AI companies competing with foundation models also have a cloud business or have partnered with a top cloud company. The training is done by these companies at a huge cost, and the AI is available as an API accessible over the Internet for inference. The foundation model cannot be used directly to build intelligent applications. There is fine-tuning needed with your data for your industry vertical before you can build your intelligent application.

You can still access the API on the cloud and keep your data protected.

ChatGPT is built on the GPT-3.5 model, which has trained data till September 21st only. Enterprise can use ChatGPT with its data in two ways:

A. Add the data in the prompt itself.

B. Point to a data source in your prompt by calling a cognitive search function.

This approach keeps the data in the instance of the chatbot built upon a foundation model like GPT or BARD.

Calling for Innovation: I foresee more enterprise platforms adding technology modules for enterprise support for prompt engineering and support for data ingestion for context-aware chatbots.

Another possibility is that the inference Generative AI moves to the edge of a device or vehicle similar to how we got TinyML for mobile. This would require more processing power on the edge, but that is happening too and calling for your innovation.

12.2.3 Understanding costs

There is the huge cost of training which is borne by the companies building the foundation models. The next cost is simply to run the foundation model in inference. Or to access the model as an API and fine-tune it with your data, which is also a training cost.

OpenAI offers a pricing based on tokens similar to the cloud business model today. A token is a set of characters that make up words, including spaces. Developers can tokenize text using the transformers package in Python or the gpt-3-encoder package in Node.js. Token pricing is based on per 1000 tokens. You can fine-tune existing models with your data to build out intelligent applications. The data you use determines your price. Open AI offers four different models, Ada, Babbage, Curie, and DaVinci, and each of these different models comes with a different cost per 1K/tokens. A token is a piece of a word and is not exactly a breakdown of words but includes spaces and could be parts of a word from your training data of sentences and paragraphs. According to OpenAI, 1000 tokens is about 750 words, or a typical paragraph, such as this one you are reading, is about 35 tokens. It is important to understand the cost of training for fine-tuning and to select the right model to fine-tune the model with your data. For example, DaVinci costs 3 cents (or $0.03) per 1K tokens. After your model is ready for inference or customer or event internal pilot testing, there is a separate cost for usage, which again for DaVinci comes to 12 cents (or $0.12) per 1K tokens.

There are tools available to keep check on how many tokens you have and what it costs for training or usage.

For example, OpenAI offers the tool "tokenizer" to track the costs of tokens.

12.3 Which Enterprise Industries Have Opportunities and Challenges with Generative AI

What industries will be impacted by generative AI and why?

Let's look at industries by different categories based on what modality of data they have.

12.3.1 Industries with lots of text data

Some industries use text as a customer touch point. Examples of these are education, courts/lawyers, writers, journalists, and copy editors. Generating text is co-related to value creation or cost reduction in these industries. So they are at the forefront of examples we see about ChatGPT and BARD.

12.3.2 Industries with lots of numbers

Finance, weather, health informatics, and energy usage are all rich in lots of data from historic data and also continue to generate data in time series. These industries lend themselves to applying machine learning to their data. They could also be used to do fine-tuning of a foundation model using their data for semi-supervised learning to build out new applications.

Call for Innovation: This is where enterprises will continue to use machine learning for solving existing problems by creating efficiencies. It also calls for innovative thinking to develop use cases where machine learning has hit its limitation, and there could be use cases that can be solved by semi-supervised learning applied on top of a foundation model.

12.3.3 Industries with lots of visual data

These are industries that use lots of cameras and collect images, faces, and videos. These images can be used to recognize faces or do fine-tuning of an image generation foundation model. So the application of recognizing faces for identity in airports, factories will benefit from this. Companies in this category that use image generation for value creation, such as generating ad copy, advertisement, or images of famous people or images for education will benefit and be impacted by automating some human-led jobs using generative AI.

12.4 Generative AI in Automated Building

I asked BARD, the intelligence chatbot search engine from Google, a question, and here is the poem it gave me. This gives me hope as I explore the social implication of generative AI and intelligent chatbots that has taken over our collective attention and raises questions about society, legality, inclusion, and ethics.

"Why is your name Bard?"

I can't sing in the traditional sense, but I can generate text that sounds like a song. For example, I could generate a song about the adventures of a bard or a song about the beauty of nature. I could also generate a song that is simply meant to be entertaining or funny.

Here is an example of a song that it generated:

> I am a bard, a teller of tales,
> I sing of heroes and their battles.
> I know the stories of kings and queens,
> And the legends of gods and monsters.
> I travel from town to town,
> Singing my songs for all to hear.
> I bring joy to the hearts of the people,
> And hope for their souls.
> I am a bard, a keeper of stories,
> I will never let them be forgotten.
> I will sing them until the end of time,
> And beyond.

Increasingly, a large percentage of content on the Internet is becoming AI-generated. Manon Den Dunnen has warned us about the impact of this content on the psychological impact of how we are going toward distrusting all information because of fake data.

OpenAI's CEO shared ChatGPT's growth at the New York Times DealBook Summit in December 2024 that ChatGPT has grown to have 300 million people using it weekly, and they are making 1 billion chat messages daily. These are people who have taken time away from their engagement on social media and e-commerce and their regular lives from consuming content to generating content via ChatGPT.

In the 1990s, we saw an explosion of user-generated content with the advent of wikis and comments on websites, which later led to social networks and messaging platforms. Jeremiah Owyang had formulated Foresters' psychographic profiles based on people's propensity to just read or add likes or add comments or full blog posts on the Internet. With social networks, smart phones, and messaging, this shifted with a generation of users who created visual and emoji content. Now we are at the cusp of users' generative content again but are getting creative to prompt the generative AI to generate poems, search responses, stories and comics, and code in the case of developers and some students.

Developers who would never stop to read poetry are creating prompts for ChatGPT to create poetry and marveling at its rhyming and ability to generate age-appropriate content.

All the hype is about ChatGPT writing poetry and stories, etc. But it is not engaging us one way by inviting us to watch its stories and poems. It is responding to human prompts to generate these and doing so. I see a social shift in the making with us humans excited with a new toy; we can engage to light a new fire. It is calling for our imagination and partnership with AI. Much research needs to be done by psychologists, social scientists, and anthropologists to help us understand this shift and connect it to our past and lead us into the future.

With AI development, it is clear that AI that is ethical and works for all of us requires a diverse group of people to be involved in the development cycle. With generative AI, this has been extended to bring AI as a collaborator into the diverse team. It is left to us whether we are going to use this fire to set the world on fire or use it as a spark to ignite new paths. I would like to end with a quote by Jay Z: "We don't just shine, we illuminate the whole show." The show has just begun and is waiting for you!

SECTION THREE

Responsible GenAI and Societal Impact

13

Ethical Responsible GenAI

State of Research of Ethical Responsible GenAI

Do you know what the difference is between AI ethics and responsible AI? Responsible AI is a framework that companies have created as a guidepost to build AI that is human-centered, trustworthy, and built by multi-disciplinary teams from start to finish.

An excellent example of responsible AI comes from Diya Wynn, the Responsible AI Practice Lead of Amazon AWS. "Responsible AI is an approach that encompasses people, process and technology that supports the design, build and operations of AI systems that minimizes risk and unintended impact while maximizing benefits." (WeeklyWed Series, 2025, YouTube)

Wael Mahmoud of Airbnb talks about the five pillars of responsible AI as "fairness (equal and just treatment), transparency & explainability (understanding decision-making processes), accountability (clear mechanisms for responsibility), privacy & security (data protection), and robustness (resilience to challenges)" (Shergadwala, 2025).

There are five key elements across all responsible AI frameworks. These are data privacy, security, inclusion, fairness, and inference scaling.

1. Data privacy when building AI responsibly comes to designing AI in a privacy-preserving way.
2. Security is about data protection from access not only by the outside world and ensuring the right access controls are in place for privacy by design and differential privacy.
3. Inclusion is about making sure that the AI does not leave out a segment of stakeholders or hurt someone unintentionally.

DOI: 10.1201/9788743808145-16

4. Fairness is about bias detection, mitigation. It has evolved with several metrics to ensure that the AI is fair and unbiased without giving preferential treatment to one segment of users in its underlying data.

5. Inference scaling is about the optimal allocation of resources for an LLM to run inference in the production version of the AI. This is to ensure the balance between accuracy and computation resources, such as tokens required to run inference. This is critical because too many tokens will be costly for the customer and also for reducing the impact on the environment, as we are aware of the cost of running an LLM on our land, water, and forest resources (Wu et al., 2024).

13.1 Ownership

AI in general has been criticized for being biased and not inclusive, reflecting biases of society from the training data collected by the people who build it in technology companies.

Fairness: Generative AI exacerbates this bias further because it is trained on huge volumes of data from the Internet with all its quirky and unrelieved contents. Additionally, generative AI has been trained by several new companies from data they did not get permission from the owners. One such example is Stability AI, which built stable diffusion for image generation and is being sued by Getty Images for training its diffusion model using Getty images, so much so that the generated images show a Getty image watermark. The trained images of the Chinese generative AI model Taiyi show Chinese people, while the image generation models built by Stable Diffusion and Midjourney are limited to their trained images.

Fairness analyzer metrics, such as those from IBM 360, are not available for generative AI. This is an opportunity that calls for innovators to build fairness metrics and tools to test and reduce bias for generative models.

Trust and explainability: This raises trustworthiness concerns about content generated on whether companies can use the generated images for their ad creatives or presentations or whether they risk the liability of a lawsuit from the content owners.

As of the writing of this book, ChatGPT has held the trust of users despite its NLP hallucinations that lead to nonfactual generated answers.

Enterprise users using GPT models or APIs such a PalM will not be as accepting of reducing the liability for their businesses. This calls for explainability for generative AI models. Again, I see an opportunity for innovators to define what explainability for a generative model looks like and how to make it work for their planned use of generative AI. The same is applicable for code generation models as they were trained on open-source code from GitHub, raising questions of ownership of the underlying code. Again, there is an opportunity for developers to build tools to validate the accuracy and legitimacy of generated code.

Accountability: As more startups build out new middleware models upon the foundation models who have built their models at extensive costs with huge volumes of data and billions of parameters, it is not clear how the companies who built their models out of code or images they do not own will be held accountable with pending lawsuits.

As a business owner of data in companies, when you use generative AI models, you cannot hide behind them being non-transparent or biased today, as that will shift the data liability to your company in the future. Some companies like Adobe have introduced generative AI in their product portfolio and are evaluating how to create a business model to compensate the artist whose work contributed to training the models that generate images.

I would urge you to think about this from the cost of value creation perspective. Would it be fair, and is it sustainable, to assume that artists will accept a portion of their current compensation by creating art to become training data for AI to generate images to be used by their customers, replacing them with generative AI? This seems far into the future but appears to be an inevitable path of cannibalizing existing artists' work. Concept Art Association is one organization pushing back on the unethical practices of companies like Stability AI for using artists' work without compensation. This is an open issue of training data ownership that is unethical and is still unresolved.

13.1.1 Security

ChatGPT has been shown to be susceptible to adversarial attack, allowing for it to be manipulated by anyone who uses misleading information to misguide its output. This is a huge open area that needs more work. The key is to look at data that you share when talking to intelligent apps and be aware of whether your data can be saved by the model to be used for training the model, compromising your data ownership and protection. Pamela Gupta, NIST advisor, has written about the top three Cybersecurity risks with Generative AI. Look at the Reference section of her article.

Call for Innovation: Look for ways to provide data to the AI but keep the AI securely in creative ways of storage, access, permission layers that can be dynamically checked, etc.

13.1.2 Equity

Equity is the concept of giving access to everyone, especially making it easy for someone who has less access to something. AI ethicist Susanna Raj has posted her testing of ChatGPT to generate documents needed for a startup. It is not easy for any new entrepreneur to learn how to do it and where to go to get this knowledge. This is true of several other people and situations. Students in rural areas or international students may not know about studying options that a local or city student may know. A tourist to a new place may be intimidated by many commute options and not know where to find out how to get a bus pass for mobility in a new place. People trying out new careers with no guidance may not know where to begin, and this is common with people who pívot even mid-career to new passions. All of these and more need access to information and have used search engines historically. ChatGPT, with its context-aware chat, made it accessible to common people with its human-centric chat capability, and that has contributed to equitable access to information and a huge scale of adoption. I would caveat this with the concern about the accuracy of the answers provided by ChatGPT and if that can be improved with some explainability citing sources. Then, it would be reliable and continue to democratize access to information equitably.

13.2 Automation and How It Affects Your Jobs

Let us look at what jobs are affected by generative AI, specifically ChatGPT and such intelligent applications of text-based modalities.

Schools that teach students to learn by rote or write just by fetching information from the Internet will find students using ChatGPT, and once search has such a chatbot integrated, it will become mainstream to search and get answers and not go to school for such an education. So education that teaches students critical thinking and applying the learning will become important. Elizabeth Losh, Director of the Equality Lab, Professor of English and American Studies at The College of William and Mary, said this at a Rutgers University event about Generative AI. "We want our students to be interpretive, risky writers." Here, risky writers mean they think for themselves and create writing that is interpretive like art. Such learning has creativity and the unique fingerprint of the human in their writing, which is reflective of their experience, emotions, and beliefs. Education that does not create such thinkers who can communicate will be challenged by such generative AI-based intelligent applications.

On the other hand, developers who can comprehend the need and have the imagination to create the middleware to create different flavors of intelligent app personalities that can produce a variety of risk levels of writing will create new jobs and products.

Lawyers will be challenged to get more creative instead of finding citations of past case precedences.

Business development managers will have to be creative to understand how to create value and what these value drivers are. This requires a shift in business leadership roles to be tech and data savvy but be innovative to create and test new business models. In the data economy, data has been pedaled as currency for the past 20 years, and partnerships have been forged by trading customer data. In the new evolving world order with generative AI data models, a pre-trained model is used to generate content. This content creates value for the customer by gleaming new knowledge from the new data. So the business acumen of the business leader who understands the business and which data can make the AI smarter will help them grow better in their career.

13.2.1 Augmented workforce

Image artists and writing jobs: I would predict that artists and writers of creative work cannot be replaced by generative AI, but the AI will become a tool for augmentation in the hands of the artists who adapt to learn prompt engineering to make the AI enhance their work.

For music, generative AI models such as Music ML can create music with technical competency. The film industry has begun using generated voices already, and this is not welcome news for voice actors or book readers. But creative music and art are created by artists as a manifestation of their emotions, and humankind has created art as an expression of their lived experiences, and this will not go away. The generative AI will augment musicians with tools and augment to help them with their work and cannot create music with emotions.

One example of this is when generative AI was used to create a song in the voice of an artist who didn't sing the original song. It sounds like the artist's voice, and the music is bearable, but it lacks emotions and cannot be used or called art.

As we sift through daily news articles, blogs, and YouTube videos of enthusiasts showing how generative AI is replacing the job of marketing writers, or musicians or artists and poets, I would say that only the people who are marketers, musicians, artists, and poets can speak to the quality of the generated content. These real people and their work are needed to train the AI, so I do not see these jobs replaced but their roles evolving with AI as a tool to create an augmented workforce.

13.3 Explainability Bias

Explainability or transparency is lacking in generative AI. The work by Nagisetty et al. (2020) covers it, but this topic is in the early stages.

> **Call for Innovation:** This is an open field with a creative approach to creating transparency and explainability for generative AI.

13.4 Legal Issues

Who owns code generated by an AI?

Who owns the generated content? Can it be copyrighted?

What is the liability for stolen content upon which a model is built?

All these questions are open, and there are several legal cases on the stability of AI, as mentioned earlier.

References

WeeklyWed Series. (2025, March 10). Responsible AI Practice with Diya Wynn [Video]. YouTube. https://www.youtube.com/live/Io7-Dk8m5ig

Shergadwala, M. (2025, February 24). Takeaways from Mahmoud's talk on Operationalizing Responsible AI. Medium. https://medium.com/@murtuza.shergadwala/takeaways-from-mahmouds-talk-on-operationalizing-responsible-ai-62548fc40ccb

Nagisetty, V., Graves, L., Scott, J., & Ganesh, V. (2020). XAI-GAN: Enhancing Generative Adversarial Networks via Explainable AI Systems. ArXiv. https://arxiv.org/abs/2002.10438

Wu, Y., Sun, Z., Li, S., Welleck, S., & Yang, Y. (2024). Inference Scaling Laws: An Empirical Analysis of Compute-Optimal Inference for Problem-Solving with Language Models. ArXiv. https://arxiv.org/abs/2408.00724

14

AI and Social Change

14.1 Anthropomorphism

People are sitting in front of ChatGPT like the mirror of Erised[1] asking it all kinds of questions. The worst part, in my opinion is, they want to believe the answers.

In the early days of the World Wide Web, there used to be a joke: "You do not know on the internet if you are talking to a dog." This is not relevant today because dogs (and cats)[2] have Twitter accounts. But the meaning behind that statement is to challenge believing information from the Internet. We go to search engines and look for anything and everything and use it to argue what is right because Google said so. However, search engines fetched websites were built by humans, so the information they brought could be pointed to a human even if they were a dishonest one. Now, when we know the AI is generating answers and it is fetching them from its memory of billions of neurons from its training data, which is the same content of the entire Internet, why are we alarmed?

The reason is that the search engines led us to the website to verify for ourselves, which ChatGPT-like chatbots do not lead us to. But I would argue that the more important factor is that we, as humans, anthropomorphize the generative AI chatbot.

Anthropomorphology has been well researched in social sciences. It is when a person humanizes something that is not human. For example, we project our emotions on our pets, or the famous example is the doctor ball Nelson in Castaway movie.

1 https://harrypotter.fandom.com/wiki/Mirror_of_Erised

2 https://twitter.com/MoetBlindCat

DOI: 10.1201/9788743808145-17

There are three primary reasons. One is that it looks like a human face so we want to be friends with it, and we cannot explain its unpredictable behavior, says Nicholas Epley, a professor of behavioral science at the University of Chicago. "No other species has this tendency." Epley is the author of Mindwise: How We Understand What Others Think, Believe, Feel, and Want (see reference). Second is the psychology of attribution to nonhuman objects, and third is our drive for connection, and the lonelier we are, the more we humanize non-objects more.

This raises the question and calls for future research on whether ChatGPT-like generative AI chatbots will isolate people to chat with the AI, get lonely and anthropomorphize it and get attached, believe its prediction, be blind to its limitations, and change society to become more lonely and dependent on the AI.

The iPhone created a generation of kids pinching magazine papers, social media created a generation of teens with mental health issues believing everyone is better than them. What will ChatGPT create within a generation chatting with an AI, trusting it and isolating themselves more?

14.2 Voice Clone and Deepfakes

Voice clone is the technology of generating a voice that is a replica of another human voice. This comes under the category of deepfakes as it creates fake voices of people. This has created an ethical uproar when celebrity voices are cloned and used instead of paying them and asking for permission to use their voice.

There are three main ethical considerations when using voice clones

1. Accuracy

   You are responsible as the user to playback the audio and check if everything is correct. Let us not get carried away by the awe of how AI is generating a human-sounding voice and conversation. That is amazing, but the content should be factually correct.

   Who can verify it?

   Anyone who understands their business and customers can validate whether what the AI-generated podcaster is talking about makes sense and is factual.

   AI has shown made-up citations, so watch out if it lists research papers (Huang et al., 2023).

2. Deepfake audio
   Audio generation is a double-edged sword, like all technologies. When AI makes a podcast, is the audio creating a sound-alike of some existing or famous person? Do you have the right to emulate that person? Is it ethical? Think about the morality of this and also the business risks it brings to your company.

3. Blind dependency
   How do we make sure we are not completely relying on this technology to do the job of us humans? What part of the technology is adding value, and what is making us lazy and dependent on AI?

Is the podcast showing bias in how it brings gender-bias or patriarchy in tones or implied bias in the personas created in the podcast? Check this without blindly trusting the technology.

14.3 Competencies Needed for Success in the Generative AI Ecosystem

For developers and product managers:

- understanding of capabilities and limitations of models;
- comparison of models on what fits your business or product ideas;
- creativity to create new products that solve gaps evolving in the ecosystem;
- API based modeling;
- API product management for developer platforms;
- ability to be innovative without losing ethics;
- privacy-preserving products.

For business leaders:

- understanding pricing strategies for yet-to-be-deployed products;
- data knowledge to build partnerships;
- smartness to ask strategy questions with an in-depth understanding of AI research, e.g., Impact on business if the underlying model is retrained;

- data ownership and privacy-preserving policies for different markets.

For software developers:

- proficiency in programming languages and frameworks commonly used for building generative AI models, such as TensorFlow, Keras, and PyTorch;
- knowledge of data structures and algorithms, as well as statistical and mathematical concepts that are relevant to machine learning and AI;
- familiarity with cloud computing platforms and distributed computing systems for training and deploying AI models at scale;
- ability to work with large datasets and pre-processing techniques like data cleaning, feature engineering, and data augmentation;
- experience with neural architecture search and hyperparameter tuning techniques to optimize the performance of AI models.

For product managers:

- deep understanding of the market and customer needs for AI-powered products and services;
- knowledge of data analytics and metrics to measure the success of AI-powered products and services.

For business managers:

- ability to collaborate effectively with technical and non-technical stakeholders across the enterprise, including data scientists, software developers, business analysts, legal and compliance teams, and executive leadership;
- understanding of the strategic value and potential applications of generative AI within the enterprise context, including opportunities for automation, optimization, and innovation;
- familiarity with the technical concepts and terminology related to generative AI, such as machine learning, deep learning, natural language processing, computer vision, and reinforcement learning;

- ability to identify and evaluate use cases for generative AI within the enterprise, considering factors such as feasibility, scalability, impact, and ROI;
- knowledge of the data and infrastructure requirements for implementing generative AI solutions within the enterprise, including considerations such as data governance, security, and compliance;
- understanding of the ethical and social implications of generative AI, including potential biases, risks, and regulatory requirements.

For product managers, business managers, and software developers:

- understanding ethical considerations and potential biases when developing AI models that can have a significant impact on people's lives;
- ability to collaborate with cross-functional teams and stakeholders, including developers, data scientists, UX designers, and executives;
- continuous learning and experimentation to stay up-to-date with the latest AI research and technologies, as well as emerging market trends and opportunities;
- empathy and user-centric mindset to design AI-powered products and services that deliver meaningful value to customers and end-users;
- understanding of regulatory and legal requirements for AI-powered products and services.

References

Huang, L., Yu, W., Ma, W., Zhong, W., Feng, Z., Wang, H., Chen, Q., Peng, W., Feng, X., Qin, B., & Liu, T. (2023). A Survey on Hallucination in Large Language Models: Principles, Taxonomy, Challenges, and Open Questions. ArXiv. https://doi.org/10.1145/3703155

15

Conclusion

We have seen the various technologies evolving in the generative AI space and looked at the impact on business models, markets, industries, and job roles, as well as the social impact on us as humans.

In all the promise of ChatGPT as a showcase of the possibilities of generative text, we can see consumer applications and new ways of teaching, researching, or engaging with brands as consumers. The challenge in the enterprise space has been integrating LLMs into other existing systems and getting them access to disparate, siloed data sources. Some legitimate issues need to be resolved, such as the need for middleware API layers, clarity on data ownership from generated content, and the cost of using the inference models. But what stops the enterprise short of the reality of the possibilities is not only the lack of human imagination but ethical concerns about building AI responsibly and reducing risks from training data copyright and data privacy and security issues.

The development cycle of artificial intelligence has shown that building AI that is ethical and works without bias for all of us requires a diverse set of people to be involved in the development cycle. Generative AI has extended this by creating an opportunity by bringing AI as a collaborator into the diverse team to generate content of all kinds.

The first step to get large language models to understand human speech in context has begun with its limitation of few languages and propensity to hallucinate. But the journey has begun, nonetheless. Now, we are accelerating to an inflection point in the software industry and domains such as education, search, marketing, and customer support with promises to create a cascade of change in how we engage with the machine. Mostly, it is calling for our humanity with logic and heart!

It calls for strategic product management of platforms, business leadership to create scalable business models, and AIX designing of human-computer interfaces that are inclusive, transparent, and ethical.

DOI: 10.1201/9788743808145-18

The spark is here. If you engage, you will learn and iterate and get to something bigger and better across all industries and modalities of human communication.

It is up to us whether we are going to use this spark to set the world on fire or use it to ignite new paths for everyone. This is just the beginning!

Praise For Sudha Jamthe's Books

"Sudha Jamthe's no-nonsense approach to IoT is refreshing, informative, and thorough. Read 'The Internet of Things Business Primer if you want to succeed in the IoT ecosystem.'"

– Ben Parr, Author of Captivology,
CEO of Co-founder/CMO Octane AI &
one of Inc.'s Top 10 IoT Experts.

"Sudha brings case studies from IoT Entrepreneurs and Product Builders globally and combines them with in-depth analysis from her own experience with Mobile Products to offer a must-read book about how to build a successful IoT Business. Watch out; this is one of those books you are going to read and reread many times to serve as your bible as the IoT ecosystem shapes out over the next few years."

– Myles Weissleder, SF NewTech Meetup Founder.

"'The Internet of Things Business Primer' is a guidebook for innovators, entrepreneurs, and technology leaders looking for practical examples of best practices to build a successful IoT business. Sudha brings her own experience and the one of other entrepreneurs that have had a meaningful impact on charting the path of the IoT industry"

– Davide Vigano, CEO Sensoria Inc.

"Analysis of IoT from a business perspective by a seasoned business and product leader – that is what this book is all about. Sudha has done an amazing job in evaluating IoT and has shown us how to make a business out of it. This is not an easy task, and Sudha has done complete justice to it."

– Pragati Rai, Sr Innovation specialist Deutsche Bank & Author Android Application Security Essentials.

"Sudha is an amazing thought leader in the new and exciting field of IoT. She is talented and inspiring with her words and work. It's exciting to see her put her deep knowledge of IoT and sharp vision of the future of this trend of technology into this book."

– Ahmed Banafa, Professor, San Jose State University.

"We live in a connected world that continues to evolve each day. Therein lies the opportunity to build a business. Sudha Jamthe brings her years of experience as a technologist to this comprehensive guide, applying her own experience and drawing from others in case studies that solidify important concepts. *The Internet of Things Business Primer* is the definitive source for anyone looking to blaze a path in the IoT world and be successful doing it."

– Frank Gruber CEO and Cofounder of Tech.co and Author Startup Mixology.

"Sudha Jamthe's new book provides the definitive roadmap for building an IoT business and navigating the forthcoming disruption across many industries with a comprehensive overview covering technology, business models and use cases"

– Ajit Jaokar, Author of Data Science for IoT and CEO of Futuretext.

"I really enjoyed Sudha's first book 'IoT Disruptions' that covers the universe of opportunities that IoT is bringing to our lives. This book 'The Internet of Things Business Primer' goes deeper to offer an in-depth guide and case studies for anyone who wants to learn how to build an IoT Business to accelerate the digital transformation."

– Josep Clotet, Founding Managing Director,
Barcelona Technology School.

"Sudha is a great supporter of the grassroots of Silicon Valley. I had the honor to work with her when developing Startup Weekend back in 2010 with eBay and PayPal. In this book, Sudha is leveraging her unique insight to prepare the next wave of innovation and support the IoT community. This is not another book about IoT, this is a map on how to navigate the future of IoT entrepreneurship,"

– Franck Nouyrigat. Co-founder of
Global Startup Weekend and Partner at recorp

"I have known Sudha for many years, and she is highly respected for her insights in developing products for the 21st century. She really is a visionary, able to spot new technology trends in the social and mobile arenas. Read her book slowly and digest her advice. I suspect you will refer back to it many times"

– Brian Solis, Principal Analyst,
Altimeter Group, a Prophet company.

Appendix 1

Shortlist of Generative AI Models

1. BERT
2. GPT-3 and GPT-4
3. Imagen
4. DALL-E
5. No Language Left Behind (NLLB-200)
6. Ada
7. Babbage
8. Curie
9. DaVinci
10. Tencent's Different
11. Dimension Me
12. LaMDA
13. Flan-T5
14. GPT-4
15. Gemini (prior BERT)
16. Alibaba's QwQ-Max
17. Hunyuan Turbo S
18. GPT-4o
19. Claude 3.5 Sonnet
20. DeepSeek V3
21. LLAMA models (from Meta)

Appendix 2

Research & References

Here are reference links to papers and learning material on topics referenced in this book.

You can also follow generativeaibook.org for more up-to-date information on the Generative AI space.

ChatGPT

ChatGPT Growth is the fastest-growing app on the Internet at 100 million users in 2 months in January 2023. https://www.reuters.com/technology/chatgpt-sets-record-fastest-growing-user-base-analyst-note-2023-02-01/

ChatGPT supports 95 languages: https://seo.ai/blog/how-many-languages-does-chatgpt-support#:~:text=ChatGPT

Microsoft invests $10B in OpenAI (news)

Cost of Search Business vs ChatGPT-based search

https://www.semianalysis.com/p/peeling-the-onions-layers-large-language

Kinsa Stats on Search Engine Market Share https://kinsta.com/search-engine-market-share/

https://www.bloomberg.com/news/articles/2023-01-23/microsoft-makes-multibillion-dollar-investment-in-openai

https://www.technologyreview.com/2022/09/14/1059481/baidu-chinese-image-ai-tiananmen/

https://techcrunch.com/2022/12/31/how-china-is-building-a-parallel-generative-ai-universe/'

https://aibusiness.com/ml/there-s-no-such-thing-as-generative-ai-

https://www.analyticsinsight.net/enterprise-ai-vs-generative-ai-key-difference-and-benefits/

AI Hallucinations

https://aclanthology.org/2022.naacl-main.387.pdf (On the Origin of Hallucinations in Conversational Models: Is it the Datasets or the Models? Nouha Dziri† ◊ Sivan Milton‡ Mo Yu¶ Osmar Zaiane† Siva Reddy◊ ‡ †University of Alberta ◊Mila – Quebec AI Institute ‡McGill University ¶ IBM Research dziri@cs.ualberta.ca)

Generative AI Technical Models

- https://www.narrativa.com/flan-t5-a-yummy-model-superior-to-gpt-3/#:~:text=T5%20consists%20of%20transformer%2Dbased,natural%20language%20processing%20(NLP).
- No Language Left Behind (NLLB) (Sparse Mixture-of-Experts model) https://ai.facebook.com/research/no-language-left-behind/
- SQuad 2.0 model from Stanford https://web.stanford.edu/class/archive/cs/cs224n/cs224n.1194/reports/default/15843151.pdf
- https://github.com/facebookresearch/fairseq/tree/nllb
- PaLm explained https://medium.datadriveninvestor.com/pathways-language-model-palm-df4b725411fc

Comparison between BERT and GPT models

https://blog.invgate.com/gpt-3-vs-bert#:~:text=Differences%20between%20GPT%2D3%20and%20BERT&text=While%20GPT%2D3%20only%20considers,sentence%20or%20phrase%20is%20essential

Industry Applications

https://www.automatedbuildings.com/2023/02/09/imagining-generative-ai-in-the-automated-building-world/

Tools

Creating Annotated Corpora for diverse languages New NLP Lab at Princeton http://newnlp.princeton.edu/

Bring ChatGPT into Excel - An example of integration https://www.youtube.com/watch?v=kQPUWryXwag

Chatbot metrics https://www.freshworks.com/live-chat-software/chatbots/chatbot-analytics/

The Advanced Prompt Generator Template Tool by Borriss: https://borriss.gumroad.com/l/APW

Music Generation AI
Music ML - https://google-research.github.io/seanet/musiclm/examples/
Riffusion Music Model explained - https://www.riffusion.com/about
Stable Diffusion-Based Models (open source)
ControlNet https://arxiv.org/abs/2302.05543
Scribble Diffusion (built upon ControlNet)

Prompt engineering
Prompt writer tool: https://borriss.gumroad.com/l/APW
Prompt Guide for Music - scroll down to the bottom: https://www.riffusion.com/about
Prompt Engineering Guide for Product Developers - https://www.promptingguide.ai/risks/adversarial
Learning Prompt engineering free course - https://learnprompting.org/
Tools for prompt engineering as PromptSource and OpenPrompt
Chain of Prompt Reasoning https://ai.googleblog.com/2022/05/language-models-perform-reasoning-via.html?m=1

Generative AI Timeline
List of models over time: https://www.fabianmosele.com/ai-timeline
GPT4 Integration into Khan Academy - Education example https://blog.khanacademy.org/harnessing-ai-so-that-all-students-benefit-a-nonprofit-approach-for-equal-access/
ChatGPT enhanced homework https://uoft-csc413.github.io/2023/assets/assignments/a1.pdf
https://google-research.github.io/seanet/musiclm/examples/
Generated Viral Music copying Drake and Weekend controversy https://www.linkedin.com/news/story/ai-song-sounds-an-alarm-in-music-6261850/
Language AI references
GPT- SW3 Swedish language https://www.ai.se/en/node/81535/gpt-sw3
GPT-3 for languages of India - www.AI4Bharat.org
GPT-3 for African languages - Masakhane Group (Masakhane.io) and Lanfrica (lanfrica.com/)

Research papers

Bommasani, Rishi, et al. "On the Opportunities and Risks of Foundation Models." ArXiv.org, 12 July 2022, https://arxiv.org/abs/2108.07258.
Lester, B., Al-Rfou, R., & Constant, N. (2021). The Power of Scale for Parameter-Efficient Prompt Tuning.

Goodfellow, Ian, Generative Adversarial Networks (2014) https://arxiv.org/abs/1406.2661

Khashabi, D., Lyu, S., Min, S., Qin, L., Richardson, K., Welleck, S., Hajishirzi, H., Khot, T., Sabharwal, A., Singh, S., & Choi, Y. (2021). Prompt Waywardness: The Curious Case of Discretized Interpretation of Continuous Prompts.

Prompt engineering "let's think step by step" Large Language Models are Zero-Shot Reasoners https://arxiv.org/abs/2205.11916.

PaLM model paper https://arxiv.org/abs/2204.02311 (PaLM)

Generative AI and Cybersecurity and Data Safety

Data Diva talks about Data Privacy and ChatGPT https://www.linkedin.com/pulse/chatgpt-large-language-models-llms-data-privacy-what-need-reynolds/

3 risks about ChatGPT and Generative AI by Pamela Gupta https://www.linkedin.com/pulse/3-risks-you-should-know-generative-ai-chatgpt-business-pamela-gupta/

Cost of Tokens for using Foundation Models from Open AI

Tech tool to measure how many tokens you need: https://platform.openai.com/tokenizer

Developers can tokenize text using the transformers package in Python or the gpt-3-encoder package in Node.js.

Generative AI Investor Landscape by Kevin Mu (investor) https://www.linkedin.com/feed/update/urn:li:activity:7039250607924269056/

https://news.artnet.com/art-world/getty-images-suing-stability-ai-stable-diffusion-illegally-scraped-images-copyright-infringement-2243631#:~:-text=Stable%20Diffusion%20and%20other%20A.I.,said%20it%20violates%20their%20copyrights.

Cost of Training Models

Stanford researchers cloned GPT AI for $600 and had to pull it out of open source because of terms of service - Alpaca AI https://interestingengineering.com/innovation/stanford-researchers-clone-chatgpt-ai

https://ai.googleblog.com/2022/05/language-models-perform-reasoning-via.html?m=1

Visual Hallucination https://paperswithcode.com/paper/visual-chatgpt-talking-drawing-and-editing

http://www.svcl.ucsd.edu/publications/conference/2022/valhalla/main.pdf

Appendix 3

GenAI Ethical Governance References

1. The European Union's (EU) AI Act
2. Africa AI Roundtable from WorldBank https://www.worldbank.org/en/events/2024/09/21/africa-ai-governance-roundtable-bridging-north-south-perspectives-for-inclusive-ai
3. Regulatory Mapping on Artificial Intelligence in LATIN America (By Access Now) July 2024 https://www.accessnow.org/wp-content/uploads/2024/07/TRF-LAC-Reporte-Regional-IA-JUN-2024-V3.pdf
4. Continental African Strategy (African Union)

Bommasani, Rishi, et al. "On the Opportunities and Risks of Foundation Models." ArXiv.org, 12 July 2022, https://arxiv.org/abs/2108.07258.

Lester, B., Al-Rfou, R., & Constant, N. (2021). The Power of Scale for Parameter-Efficient Prompt Tuning.

Khashabi, D., Lyu, S., Min, S., Qin, L., Richardson, K., Welleck, S., Hajishirzi, H., Khot, T., Sabharwal, A., Singh, S., & Choi, Y. (2021). Prompt Waywardness: The Curious Case of Discretized Interpretation of Continuous Prompts.

Prompt engineering "let's think step by step" Large Language Models are Zero-Shot Reasoners https://arxiv.org/abs/2205.11916.

PaLM model paper https://arxiv.org/abs/2204.02311 (PaLM)

Generative AI and Cybersecurity and Data Safety

Data Diva talks about Data Privacy and ChatGPT https://www.linkedin.com/pulse/chatgpt-large-language-models-llms-data-privacy-what-need-reynolds/

3 risks about ChatGPT and Generative AI by Pamela Gupta https://www.linkedin.com/pulse/3-risks-you-should-know-generative-ai-chatgpt-business-pamela-gupta/

Cost of Tokens for using Foundation Models from Open AI

Tech tool to measure how many tokens you need: https://platform.openai.com/tokenizer

Developers can tokenize text using the transformers package in Python or the gpt-3-encoder package in Node.js.

Generative AI Investor Landscape by Kevin Mu (investor) https://www.linkedin.com/feed/update/urn:li:activity:7039250607924269056/

https://news.artnet.com/art-world/getty-images-suing-stability-ai-stable-diffusion-illegally-scraped-images-copyright-infringement-2243631#:~:text=Stable%20Diffusion%20and%20other%20A.I.,said%20it%20violates%20their%20copyrights.

Cost of Training Models

Stanford researchers cloned GPT AI for $600 and had to pull it out of open source because of terms of service - Alpaca AI https://interestingengineering.com/innovation/stanford-researchers-clone-chatgpt-ai

https://ai.googleblog.com/2022/05/language-models-perform-reasoning-via.html?m=1

Visual Hallucination https://paperswithcode.com/paper/visual-chatgpt-talking-drawing-and-editing

http://www.svcl.ucsd.edu/publications/conference/2022/valhalla/main.pdf

Index

About the Contributor

Debika Sarkar is a Software Engineer and AI Ethicist. She works as an AI Ethics Program Manager for the Business School of AI, where she researches the latest technologies within the LLM space, with a focus on making artificial intelligence more transparent, inclusive, and accessible.

She has designed and implemented AI ethics curricula for international programs, including a NeurIPS grant initiative teaching students in South Sudan to explore machine translation while preserving low-resource languages through the organization, Global South in AI. She has also advised on ethical risk assessments of AI systems, vendor accountability, and the challenges of bias and fairness in large-scale models. With a background in enterprise regulation and software development, Debika brings a combination of technical and policy expertise. She has built web applications for major clients and led workshops on responsible AI.

As the researcher of this volume, Debika brings her perspective on the intersection of technology, ethics, and language to guide readers in the rapidly evolving landscape of large language models through Sudha Jamthe's words. She is committed to ensuring that conversations about AI are not only technically rigorous but also grounded in equity, accessibility, and global context.

About the Author

Sudha Jamthe is a globally respected Technology Futurist on AI and Autonomous Vehicles with a mix of 25+ years of experience from working in the Silicon Valley technology industry, academia, and building grassroots tech ecosystems. Ms. Jamthe enjoys mentoring business leaders to innovate using no-code AI and teaches business courses focused on inclusiveness and human agency. Ms. Jamthe has developed new courses and taught AI and AI Ethics at Stanford Continuing Studies, Barcelona Technology School, and Business School of AI and is the author of seven books on IoT, Autonomous Vehicles, AI, and Generative AI. Her research focus is on inclusive AI, Autonomous Vehicles, and AIX Design. She is the chairperson of the strategic advisory board for Barcelona Technology School and an Ambassador for FundingBox Impact Connected Cars (Europe H2020) Community and NGI. She is a champion of STEM programs and Girls Who Code and host of IoT Day IoTWoman (bit.ly/iotwoman) and Global South Language AI (globalsouthinai.org) social affinity group, a US-based non-profit at NeurIPS AI conference. Jamthe has an MBA from Boston University and a B.S in Computer Science Engineering from Madras University.

She is the author of seven books, including three IoT books, "IoT Disruption," "The Internet of Things Business Primer," and "IoT Disruptions 2020"; one book on Autonomous Vehicles "2030 The Driverless World"; and two on AI, "AIX: Designing Artificial Intelligence" and "Generative AI: A Primer for Product and Business Managers." Her specialty is business model evolutions and business innovation from data. Sudha has developed and taught the "Artificial Intelligence Bootcamp: A Primer for Product and Business Managers" course at Stanford Continuing Studies Program and AI Ethics courses for four master's programs at Barcelona University. She is the founder of a global speaker series, WeeklyWed at Business School of AI her learner community to bring global practitioners and leaders shaping the world of AI to share best practices in IoT, AI, and Autonomous Vehicles space.

Sudha is a champion for STEM programs and Girls Who Code. Earlier, she served as a venture mentor at MIT and Director of Bay Area Facebook, Twitter, Pinterest, and Google+ Meetups and served as a member of (P007) IEEE global initiative on ethical considerations on the fail-safe development of autonomous and intelligent systems. She has been a guest contributor to TechCrunch, Mashable, Venturebeat, Huffington Post, Automated Buildings, TechTarget, and Axios as a respected technology futurist. She is the chair of the strategic advisory board of Barcelona Technology School, a proud member of the EU IOT Council, and an ambassador to FundingBox Impact Connected Car Europe and Next Generation Internet (NGI).

She is the co-founder of Global South in AI Inc, a non-profit organization dedicated to add inclusiveness to Language AI by training and bringing more researchers from the global south and endangered languages and hosted Global South in AI @NeurIPS2022, bringing 31 researchers.

You can reach Sudha Jamthe at sudhajamthe.com. You can follow her work at generativeaibook.org, specifically to get more resources on Generative AI, or follow her learner community at Business School of AI on LinkedIn.

For Product Safety Concerns and Information please contact our
EU representative GPSR@taylorandfrancis.com Taylor & Francis
Verlag GmbH, Kaufingerstraße 24, 80331 München, Germany